GROWING PAINS

GROWING PAINS

A PARENT'S GUIDE
to Child Development

Amanda Hill, MEd

Illustrations by Hayden Maynard

ROCKRIDGE
PRESS

For general information on our other products and services or to obtain technical support, please contact our Customer Care Department within the United States at (866) 744-2665, or outside the United States at (510) 253-0500.

Rockridge Press publishes its books in a variety of electronic and print formats. Some content that appears in print may not be available in electronic books, and vice versa.

Interior and Cover Designer: Will Mack
Art Producer: Sue Bischofberger
Editor: Lauren Ladoceour
Production Manager: Oriana Siska
Production Editor: Kurt Shulenberger

Illustrations © Hayden Maynard

ISBN: Print 978-1-64152-772-9 | eBook 978-1-64152-773-6

*To Jerry, my better half,
my one and only. There's
no one else I'd rather be
with on this wild parenting
journey than you.*

Contents

The Struggle Is Real

The morning started off with an epic breakfast meltdown. I served my preschooler French toast with maple syrup and strawberries on top—much to her obvious dismay. Through her tears, she angrily informed me that she wanted her strawberries on the side, not on top. I acknowledged her disappointment and offered to push the offending fruit onto the edge of her plate. Nope, that wasn't going to do it. She continued to cry and refused to touch her breakfast. Although this was not quite the start to my day that I had imagined, I know that this is typical behavior for a young child. I know that little ones have brains that are not yet fully developed and don't have sufficient skills to effectively manage emotions on a consistent basis. I get that episodes like this are to be expected, but that didn't make the morning drama any less unpleasant. With degrees in child development and education, in addition to many years working with children, families, and educators, I like to think that my professional background has given me a whole lot of book smarts on raising kids. Now, as a parent, I find that my children put this knowledge, as well as my patience, to the test on a daily basis.

Becoming a parent has been one of the most intensely emotional, challenging, and beautiful experiences of my life. Not only has it deepened my passion and commitment to help others understand children's development, but it has also given me a desire to teach parents and caregivers practical and effective strategies to address common behavioral challenges that arise. For nearly a decade now, I've had the opportunity to do this within my classroom as a professor of child development, as well as in parent education courses and professional development trainings for educators. I love helping parents find positive and productive ways to navigate the ever-changing landscape of raising children and the struggles that arise.

Sometimes the struggle is the meal that's not eaten (again) or getting out of the house in the morning with minimal tears. Maybe it's the incessant whining, complaining, or back talk, or the fights over brushing teeth, or the never-ending process of getting your kid to stay in bed for the night (why am I so tired at the end of the day but she is not?). Regardless of the nature of the latest challenge, there will inevitably be moments where frustration and exhaustion build, and you look at your child and think, "Ugh, I don't know how much more of this I can take!"

What I want you to know is that it's okay to feel that way. It's okay that sometimes you're irritated, overwhelmed, and exasperated during difficult moments. Even the most patient parent can be pushed to the edge by the pint-sized person he or she loves. Knowing that a behavior is developmentally typical and expected at a given age doesn't necessarily take the frustration out of it. And just because it's an anticipated behavior doesn't mean that you automatically have the tools needed to respond appropriately when it presents itself—that's what this book is for. You'll notice that each chapter is dedicated to a specific age and covers common challenges that children and parents face. My goal in writing this book is for you to find useful insights into typical behavior, as well as practical, age-appropriate, and effective strategies to utilize with your child when you need a helping hand or a fresh approach. I can't guarantee that your kid will behave perfectly or that you'll never feel frustrated again, but I can help set you on a path of peace, connection, and cooperation within your home.

The Long Game

IT ALL STARTED WITH A TRIP TO TARGET.
I was working as a nanny for three kids (ages four, five, and nine), and we were picking up a toy for a birthday party we'd be attending. When I told the youngest that he couldn't bring a coveted Transformers truck home with him, he fell to the floor in full-blown tantrum mode. As I awkwardly picked up his flailing body and tried to load him into the cart, I felt my cheeks flush and began to sweat while other shoppers stared with disapproval. Some even made remarks under their breath about how he was "out of control." The tantrum alone was overwhelming. Add to it the scrutiny of fellow shoppers, and it was downright unbearable.

Since that thrilling experience, I've learned that parents undergo this type of judgment all the time. From the moment I announced my first pregnancy, it seemed that everyone and their mother began asking questions and offering unsolicited advice. Will you be delivering vaginally or by cesarean? Will you breastfeed? Circumcise? Co-sleep? The list goes on and on. My point is this: Everyone has an opinion on how to parent, and most are more than willing to share it, whether you asked for their input or not. (And seriously, no one asked for it.)

Unfortunately, we can't stop people from offering gratuitous feedback about our children or our parenting choices. What we can do is arm ourselves with knowledge of typical child development and expected behaviors. From there, we can develop tools that will help us navigate the challenges that inevitably come with the adventure of raising kids and give us greater confidence in our parenting choices. I believe that developing a "parenting tool kit" is one of the best things we can do to drown out the noise of other people's opinions.

Monday-Morning Quarterbacks

Parenting is hard, relentless work, and we're all figuring out what shape it should take in the context of our own families. Our role as parents is not to explain our choices, our parenting styles, or even our kids' behaviors (as wild as they may be sometimes). Our role is to teach our children how to navigate the challenges that come along in life in a healthy, positive, and productive way. You are the parent of your child; you know your kid best, and you know what works for your family. To put it another way, you and your little one are on the same team, so don't let the words of Monday-morning quarterbacks get into your head for even a second.

There are many parenting perspectives and techniques, especially when it comes to dealing with behavioral challenges. Should you use rewards and punishments? Employ consequences? Use a time-out? Scold? Spank? It's easy to get lost in the mix of different ideas. Here's my best advice: Get familiar with typical child development findings and what current research tells us about kids, and then use this information as a guide as you make choices for your own family. Don't get too hung up in analysis paralysis, but rather be willing to try something new, to fail, to try again, and to adjust the strategy to meet your family's needs. Nothing is set in stone, and you will have ample opportunity to find out what works best for you and your child.

Since you are your kid's first teacher and the one who will likely be there the longest, you have the great privilege and responsibility of helping your child grow into his or her best version. You get to demonstrate tenacity by trying, falling short, and then getting back up and trying again. You get to show your child how to manage overwhelming emotions, how to ask for forgiveness when you've done something you wish you hadn't, and how to be kind, considerate, and respectful. You get to model empathy and love through your daily interactions, from kissing boo-boos and wiping bottoms to cheering loudly at soccer games and staying up late to help with the science project that's due the next day. These actions are what build a meaningful and lasting connection.

Connection is what children need more than anything. Don't get me wrong—they also seem to need 87 snacks each day and at least the same number of trips to the bathroom while stalling at bedtime. But I'm pretty confident that love and connection are at the top of the must-have list. So focus on building a healthy, respectful, and connected relationship with your child. Lead with love, and you'll be winning the game.

Where'd This Kid Come From?

Parenting provides an interesting peek into the inborn characteristics that we have as humans. During infancy, my son's regular sleeping and eating rhythms were a stark contrast to my daughter's erratic, unpredictable schedule. The juxtaposition of her intense mood with his calm demeanor highlighted some of their innate differences. Those of you with multiple children know what I mean.

The unique traits that we inherit have an impact on the way we interact with the world. Research indicates that temperament appears to be relatively stable throughout life, meaning there's no way to change a kid's natural disposition. However, we are in charge of understanding our children's temperaments and responding to their needs accordingly. The goodness of fit model, where we respect and accommodate a child's distinctive characteristics, is foundational in developing positive and effective guidance strategies.

To make things more complicated, the way temperament is exhibited often shifts as kids grow and develop. Consequently, a parenting strategy that worked well at a certain age may not be as effective the following year. For instance, a reserved and cautious four-year-old might love Mom or Dad sticking close by at a new playground until he's ready to venture out on his own. Fast forward a couple of years and this same slow-to-warm-up preteen may be appalled by a lingering parent, fearing embarrassment in front of peers. My goal is to help you better understand your child and his or her unique temperament, while also keeping typical developmental milestones in mind, so that you can develop a practical parenting tool kit that works for your family.

Before we move on, it's important to note that all developmental milestones are approximate. There is a range of what is considered typical in physical, cognitive, and social-emotional changes over time. We use these estimates as guideposts in our parenting journeys to let us know where we are and what's coming up next. To find helpful books, articles, and websites related to typical development, check out the resources at the end of this book. If you ever have questions or concerns related to your child's development, consult with a physician.

Temperament and Behavior

There is no one-size-fits-all approach to understanding behavior and emotions, which probably explains why raising a kid can be so challenging and sometimes frustrating. However, over time we get to know our children better than anyone else, and this is incredibly helpful in determining what works for them and what doesn't. Even though you might not always feel like it, you truly are the expert!

Child development professionals have long been interested in the intrinsic personality differences among children, as well as adults, and much research was done throughout the twentieth century to better understand these differences. In the late 1970s, psychiatrists Alexander Thomas and Stella Chess identified the following nine temperament traits that they believed impacted the way people respond to the world around them:

ACTIVITY LEVEL relates to how much someone is up and moving throughout the day. Some people seem to have much more energy than others. If your child routinely struggles to sit at the dinner table or seems to dance around during homework time, she likely scores higher in this category.

SENSITIVITY looks at how changes in the environment impact a person. Is your child easily bothered by certain sounds, tastes, or smells? People with high sensitivity tend to be more aware of sensory changes and can be more easily irritated. Those with a lower sensitivity threshold may be less aware of sensory changes.

REGULARITY considers routines and habits, such as sleep/wake cycles and eating patterns. If your child seems to enjoy and appreciate routine and easily follows along, he may be higher in regularity.

APPROACH AND WITHDRAWAL concern how someone reacts in new situations. Does your child resist new foods? Is she reserved when meeting new people? If so, she may score higher in this trait.

ADAPTABILITY involves how quickly or slowly your child adapts to a change in routine. If your child has a strong aversion to surprises or dislikes a disruption in his schedule, he is likely lower in adaptability. People with higher adaptability tend to have a more go-with-the-flow attitude and enjoy spontaneity.

MOOD reflects overall disposition. Some children tend to be optimistic and cheerful whereas others may be pessimistic and negative. In general, does your child seem to be cheerful or fussy?

INTENSITY reflects the amount of energy used to express emotions. Does your child burst into tears at the sight of a piece of broccoli on her plate? Does she scream with excitement when you head to the park for the afternoon? Consistent dramatic reactions, whether positive or negative, indicate higher levels of intensity.

PERSISTENCE looks at how long someone will stick with a task. Those with higher persistence levels may get locked into an activity and find it difficult to stop. If your child regularly struggles to leave enjoyable activities, like playing video games or building with toy bricks, he may have higher persistence.

DISTRACTIBILITY involves how the ability to focus is impacted by the things going on around a person. Some people can tune out a lot of distractions, whereas others are sidetracked more easily. If your child seems to have a hard time focusing when you're speaking to him or struggles to complete nightly homework, he may be higher in distractibility.

Beyond the nine traits, three main temperament types were also noted: easy/flexible, slow-to-warm-up/fearful, and difficult/feisty. Most kids fall into the easy/flexible category. They tend to be predictable in their activities and behaviors, are usually adaptable, and have a generally positive mood. Children in the slow-to-warm-up/fearful category are often given the label of shy because they take more time to adjust to new situations. Dealing with an unfamiliar setting—a new classroom or a friend's house, for example—can feel scary and overwhelming. With these children, it's best to give them time and some reassurance until they're ready to check things out for themselves. Children in the difficult/feisty category may be unpredictable, often get upset by changes in routine, and may be quick to slide into a meltdown.

Having a solid understanding of the temperament traits and types not only provides you with cues as to how to best meet your child's needs, it also gives you greater insight into your own behaviors, preferences, and emotional reactions. After all, your parenting style is affected by your own temperament as well as your child's.

Although none of these characteristics are inherently good or bad, some may be more or less desirable in certain settings. Consider, for instance, two children in a first-grade classroom. Cooper scores low in activity level, which accounts for his ability to sit and listen for lengthy periods of time. He enjoys sedentary activities and has a low degree of distractibility, providing for sustained periods of concentration. Combined with a high score in persistence, these traits allow Cooper to focus on challenging problems for extended periods of time.

By contrast, Mitchell is squirmy and active, and sitting still for more than a couple of minutes is very challenging. He prefers activities that involve plenty of large body movements. His high activity and distractibility levels, combined with a low rating in persistence, could make it a challenge for him to succeed in the traditional academic setting if proper supports aren't established. Teachers often struggle to hold his attention and find it difficult to keep him focused on class work.

Perhaps you can relate to one of the children more than the other. I, for instance, am a Cooper, through and through. My temperament made me an ideal fit in the traditional academic setting. Maybe that's you, too. Or, perhaps you relate more to Mitchell. To best assist kids like Mitchell, teachers need to accommodate these temperament characteristics within the learning environment, recognizing that these differences may necessitate a wide range of activities and teaching approaches.

My point in sharing these descriptions of temperament traits and types is to illustrate that depending on the setting, some traits and types may naturally fit better than others. What this means for us as parents is that we must spend time understanding the unique characteristics of our kids, as well as ourselves. Once we've done that, we'll be better equipped to meet our children's needs in helpful and constructive ways.

Check the Temperament Temperature

If you've never reflected on your own temperament traits or those of your child, I encourage you to try this rating exercise. Grab two different colored pens and use one to mark where you believe you fall in each category. With the other pen, indicate where you believe your child lies. To get a good grasp on your child's temperament in various settings, it may be helpful to get input from other people who regularly interact with your child.

Do you and your child have similar or different temperament traits? In what areas are you alike? In what areas are you different? How do you think this might impact your parenting style?

TEMPERAMENT SCALE

ACTIVITY LEVEL

Low Energy		High Energy

SENSITIVITY

Low		High

REGULARITY

Low Predictability		High Predictability

APPROACH AND WITHDRAWAL

Withdraws		Approaches

ADAPTABILITY

Slow to Adapt		Quick to Adapt

MOOD

Negative		Positive

INTENSITY

Less Responsive		More Responsive

PERSISTENCE

Low Persistence		High Persistence

DISTRACTIBILITY

Low Distractibility		High Distractibility

Set Realistic Goals

With both your and your child's temperaments in mind, take a couple of minutes to reflect on the following questions.

How would you honestly describe your current parenting style? It's important to have an idea of the ways in which you parent so that you can better understand the role that you play in meeting your child's needs in the way that best suits him or her. With this foundation, you can more effectively move on to the behavioral issues that you want to develop strategies for.

What behavioral issues do you want to find strategies for? Perhaps some of the following are on your list:

- ☐ Lying (page 21)
- ☐ Picky eating (page 46)
- ☐ Swear words (page 63)
- ☐ Complaining (page 86)
- ☐ Chore wars (page 100)
- ☐ Laziness (page 119)
- ☐ Body image issues (page 137)

Some of these behavioral issues can persist through several years. For instance, lying often continues in different ways throughout childhood. We'll address this for both younger children (page 21) and older kids (page 128), as the approach is a bit different depending on the age. By keeping developmental stages and the child's age in mind, we'll be better equipped to tackle challenges as they come up.

It's Okay to Say, "This Sucks!"

Throughout this book, we'll emphasize the importance of remaining calm and connected with your child so that you're teaching healthy ways to regulate emotion. However, there are many moments in parenting when intense feelings build and your emotions seem out of control—like when you've dragged yourself out of bed and whipped up home-made French toast and your kid shows her gratitude by freaking out over some misplaced berries. Feeling this way doesn't mean you're a bad parent or that you're doing things wrong. It simply means that you're human. There will be times when you're frustrated, tired, or burnt out—and that's okay. Quite frankly, there's no way around it.

In those moments when you're at your wits' end, it's best to remove yourself from the situation until you've regained your cool. Immediately pack your bags and take off for a week at a spa. Just kidding! If there's another adult around who can step in for a minute, go for a walk and get some fresh air. Let your child know that you're feeling really upset and you need some time to calm down. Realistically, we can't always escape the situation—even for just a stroll around the block, never mind a massage. In those instances, something as simple as turning on music or texting a pal to vent can help shift your mood.

The more often children witness their parents responding to challenging situations in an honest and regulated way, the greater their likelihood of exhibiting these behaviors in the future. Our children cannot do things that we do not first model for them. It's not necessary to have a poker face regarding your emotions; feelings are real, valid, and meant to be felt. The goal is to teach our children how to feel emotions while responding in an intentional and productive way.

After the heat of the moment has died down, take some time to reflect on what may have contributed to the intensity of emotions that you experienced. Consider the ways in which you respond to upsetting situations. Are there certain things that frequently set you off? How do you typically respond? It may be helpful to jot down some of the events surrounding the episode. By keeping track of highly emotional moments, you may be able to notice a pattern and then take steps toward developing a more calm and effective approach.

WHAT KIDS NOTICE

Children are perceptive and can pick up on the emotional states of others from a very early age. While still in their infancy, children begin social referencing—using emotional cues from the people around them to determine how to respond to a given situation. Smart, huh?

A couple of months ago, my daughter was riding her bike when she lost her footing and fell. My husband was with her, and he quickly but calmly ran over to scoop her up and give her a once-over. The crash had certainly startled her, and she immediately looked to her daddy to gauge his response. Had he overreacted in this moment, it might have caused her greater distress or even made it less likely that she'd hop back on two wheels.

Children look to the adults in their lives all the time to determine what responses are appropriate. This means that, as parents, we are responsible for providing children with a template for emotional regulation. We have ample opportunity to demonstrate healthy displays of emotion for our children, and seeing these healthy displays is hugely beneficial for them.

Of course, there are plenty of times when what we model is less than ideal, like last week when I yelled at my kids for emptying the contents of our pantry onto the kitchen floor, right after I had mopped it. We've all been there, and in all likelihood, we'll all find ourselves there again in the future. We're human, and this means that sometimes we make mistakes. Don't agonize over it. Simply apologize for the yelling and keep going.

4 YEAR OLDS

Look at That!

WITH A BUDDING VOCABULARY, abundant curiosity, and no filter (eek!), four-year-olds are a recipe for embarrassing and hilarious conversation. For most of my career in the preschool setting, I had horrible cystic acne, and the children I taught were quick to notice. This led to comments such as, "Miss Amanda, why are there red dots all over your face?" I wasn't the only target. A little girl once informed my colleague that his "teeth look dirty," and a young boy proclaimed that another teacher's tummy was "so big and fluffy!"

Given that I am many years removed from this setting, and much less pimple prone, I now have a greater appreciation for kids' inquisitiveness. They're processing new experiences at a swift rate, and they look to us to help them make sense of it all, even if it is at the expense of our egos.

What's New

Four-year-olds are bundles of energy, fueled by curiosity and exploration. They investigate the world around them through hands-on play. Their large body movements include activities such as running, hopping, kicking, walking easily forward and backward, and pedaling a tricycle. Their fine motor skills are improving, and they demonstrate this through tasks like getting dressed, brushing teeth, and eating successfully—albeit not always neatly—with utensils.

Children this age are egocentric, meaning that they view things largely from their own perspective and have difficulty putting themselves in another person's shoes. This may cause a kid to grab a toy out of another child's hands. At the same time, a young child who sees that Daddy burned his finger while making dinner may offer to kiss the boo-boo because she knows that makes her feel better when she gets hurt. Empathy skills improve as the brain matures and as children learn to follow our examples. Four-year-olds still have a long way to go in terms of being able to successfully manage their feelings on a regular basis, but they're certainly on their way.

Four-year-olds often love dramatic play, where they assign roles and act them out, typically with friends. Regardless of the specific theme, this type of play provides children with opportunities to engage in conflict resolution and build their self-regulatory abilities as they interact with their peers.

Capabilities and Limitations

At this age, children continue to build their vocabularies while also boosting their conversational skills. It's not uncommon to hear them happily chatting to themselves, which allows them to problem solve and work through things on their own out loud. Although they have a fairly decent mastery of grammar rules, they still make mistakes. For instance, it's common to hear things like, "I builded it!" or "He hitted me." Don't stress too much about these errors. Just continue to exhibit correct grammar usage for your little ones and they'll eventually pick it up.

Figures of speech may be challenging for preschoolers to comprehend. For instance, if you say you're "dying of hunger," your child may interpret that to mean that you'll actually die if you don't eat very soon. Part of the challenge for them may stem from their difficulty in distinguishing between fantasy and reality.

Communication

Our language has a profound influence on how we view the world, and the way we talk about our children greatly shapes the narrative they develop about themselves. The labels that we assign to our kids, as well as the ones we give ourselves, tend to work as self-fulfilling prophecies, dictating the plotlines of our lives. As kids grow, they form their identities based on the labels and language we use. When your little one empties every toy out of the bin again, you might be inclined to say, "Ugh! You're so messy!" If that's the case, disconnect the action from your child. Instead, you might say, "Oh! I see you're exploring all of your toys right now" even if what you're thinking is more like, "Lucky me, I'll get to explore them all back into the toy box tonight." When your kid reacts strongly in a situation, perhaps crying and pouting, reframe the statement "You're being too sensitive" as something like "It seems like you're feeling really upset right now." By making these subtle changes, you shift into an approach that removes labels and acknowledges feelings and behaviors.

DISCIPLINE

Throughout this book, we'll discuss age-appropriate discipline strategies for each year we move through, with every approach holding the same theme: teaching children through respectful interaction and healthy limit setting. One of the most important things you can do is calmly acknowledge your child's emotions and allow him to experience his feelings in a safe environment.

One of my current struggles with my children is leaving the park in the afternoon with minimal tears. My five-minute warning that we have to head home often results in protests and desperate pleas for more time. We've all been in this situation, and this public battle is a breeding ground for power struggles. We often end up scolding, lecturing, and cajoling our kids to comply. Unfortunately, this is rarely productive and usually just results in them continuing to climb up the play equipment until we're red-faced and sweating from trying to retrieve them.

In between the angry "do it because I said so" and the timid "please, listen to Mommy now, sweetie" is the land of firm boundaries, clear expectations, and recognition of the child's emotions. And that's where we want to be. In this case, my response to the tantrum might be, "You're disappointed that we have to leave the park because you're having so much fun." As I continue to gather our belongings, I add, "It's hard to leave fun things; you're mad that we have to leave." On good days, this is enough to calm the storm. When that's not the case, I let my child know that I will enforce the limit if she doesn't cooperate: "It looks like you're having a hard time walking to the car. You can walk over with us, or I will bring you to your seat." If my child isn't walking to the car, I follow through by picking her up and carrying her to her car seat.

In some instances, playfulness can help. If my child is moving at a sloth's pace, I might break out the silly body movements: "We're moving soooo slooooow like turtles," or "Can you hop like a bunny?" This type of redirection often piques children's curiosity and gets them moving, which can short-circuit a tantrum.

Lying

One of my favorite four-year-old tall tales comes from my work as a nanny. Ava was in her room for nap time when I heard some commotion. When I went in, she greeted me wearing a pink tutu, not the leggings and top she had been

wearing earlier. I noticed that her sheets were wet, and her pants were wadded up on the floor. I realized that she'd had an accident. Without thinking much of it, I commented, "Oh, it looks like you had an accident. Let's go get some fresh sheets." Her response was an adamant, "No, I did not!" I replied, "Yes, you did." And that, my friends, is where I went wrong. As we argued back and forth, I found myself in a battle of wills. In the midst of our argument, she went on to explain that someone had come into her room, gotten into her bed, and peed on her sheets. I wasn't buying it, of course, but she wasn't giving in.

CAUSES

Although it's beyond irritating to hear your little sweetheart lying through her teeth, take heart in knowing that it's a big developmental milestone. We just don't tend to celebrate this new skill as much as we do ones like using the toilet or riding a bike. At four years old, children have an improved theory of mind, meaning they recognize that different people may have different thoughts, beliefs, or perspectives. Combined with their creativity, imagination, and somewhat loose concept of reality and fantasy, this milestone often leads to them telling some whoppers.

Sometimes children lie because they enjoy the creative freedom of crafting their own version of events. Other times, they lie to avoid embarrassment or out of fear of getting in trouble. Regardless of the reason, lying is a rite of passage for young children and generally not something to make a huge deal about.

PREVENTION

Remind your child of the importance of honesty in a non-threatening way. For instance, you could respond to a fib with "That sounds like a wild story. Telling stories can be fun sometimes, but there are also times when it's important to tell the truth about what really happened." Cornering children and demanding that they tell the truth (as I did in the bed-wetting scenario) or using labels such as "liar" may cause shame and distrust, which in turn may lead to more lying to avoid punishment or harsh criticism in the future.

Model truth telling by being honest with your kids and other people that you interact with. Even if you think they aren't paying attention, trust me, they are.

IN THE MOMENT
With Ava, it would have been better if I had dropped the matter altogether and simply gone to get new sheets to change the bed. There was no value in proving that she did, in fact, wet the bed or in demanding that she tell me the truth. She might have been embarrassed and lied in an attempt to save face, or she might have thought it was funny to tell a make-believe story. Responding with "I wonder if you're feeling afraid to tell me that you wet the bed. Accidents happen sometimes. Let's go get those clean sheets" would have been a far better approach.

WHEN THE MOMENT HAS PASSED
By listening to what is going on underneath the surface of the lie (e.g., shame, embarrassment, fun storytelling) and modeling honesty for your child, you are helping your child establish a foundation of truth telling and openness, both of which are important in healthy relationships. It may be useful to have a conversation at a later time. For instance, I could have sat down with Ava later that day and said, "It sounded like you were telling me a story about bed-wetting, maybe because you were afraid to tell me that you'd had an accident. What would help you tell me the truth about accidents in the future?" The goal is to get a conversation going and let the child know it's safe to share with you.

In addition, continue to show appreciation for honesty by letting your child know you're glad she came to you with her news, even if it was a hard thing to share. Give her opportunities for do-overs, chances to make different choices. And more than anything, continue to remind your child that your love is unconditional; nothing will ever change that, even if she wet the bed a hundred times.

For older children who have greater cognitive skills, our response to lying is a bit different. Check out the "Lying" section (page 128).

Not Sharing

The other day I went to the grocery store to pick up a few items. Usually, I have my two children with me, so I make a mad dash around the store. This time, I had the pure bliss of shopping solo, allowing me to peruse the shelves in peace. I'd been there for about 40 minutes when a woman came up, grabbed my cart, and emptied its contents onto the floor. She quickly took off with my cart shouting, "My turn!"

Okay, so that didn't really happen. But imagine it did. You'd be appalled if it happened to you, even if you'd been there for two hours. There's no time limit on using the carts; while you're using it, it's yours. This analogy, adapted from Darla Ferris Miller's illustration in her book *Positive Child Guidance*, is one of my favorites when talking about sharing. I think it helps adults see the issue from a different perspective, one from which we can help children learn to be generous with others in a more respectful way, as opposed to forcefully requiring them to fork things over just because we say so.

CAUSES

At age four, children still struggle to put themselves in other people's shoes. They see a toy and think "I want to play with that now!", even if another child is already using it. Sometimes they act on this thought, much to the dismay of the other child. Given their developmental stage, a parental lecture on sharing or demanding that they hand toys over does little good in terms of building genuine sharing skills and concern for others.

PREVENTION

I may shock you with my advice, but here it is: Don't force your kid to share. That's right—don't do it. Making your little one hand over a toy doesn't actually teach him to share; it forces him to obey. If your boss made you give half of your lunch to a coworker, you wouldn't consider that sharing. What would true sharing look like? Offering your coworker some of your food because you know that she's hungry and you want to help.

Instead of forcing your child to share, practice model sharing and turn taking in your family. Ask your child, "Would you like some of my strawberries?" If he wants one, comment, "Here you go. I'm happy to share these with you." Also, show your appreciation when he does want to share by saying, "Thank you for sharing your snack with your brother. That was very thoughtful of you!"

When you know there might be a conflict, like when friends come to play, prep your child ahead of time. Say something like, "When Riley comes over today, you'll need to share some of your toys with her. What are some toys that you think Riley would like to play with?"

IN THE MOMENT

Even with all the modeling and prepping in the world, there will be times when your child refuses to share and even has a meltdown when asked to do so. In these instances, allow your child to use a toy until she's done with it, and help the other child find a different toy to use. "Laurie is playing with that doll right now, Riley. When she's done, you may have a turn. Let's look for some toys that are available right now." If your child has a prized possession that she never wants others to use, keep it in her bedroom. We all have items that are off-limits to others, and we keep those in special places.

WHEN THE MOMENT HAS PASSED

If things go awry, wait until your child has calmed down to talk about how to handle the situation differently next time. For instance, you might say, "Earlier today, you seemed upset when I reminded you that you needed to share with Riley. When she comes over again, what could you do differently so that you both have fun playing?" By including your child in the problem solving, you're helping her build valuable conflict resolution skills that go well beyond early childhood.

Back in my preschool teaching days, we used this approach often. We once asked the class how to deal with sharing three popular tricycles among 30 children. Some of their ideas included buying more tricycles, taking the ones from the older kids upstairs, setting a timer for turn taking, and doing one lap around the playground and then giving the next child a turn. They came up with many ideas on their own, and together we decided on one that we would try to implement, which gave them more investment in and ownership of the strategy.

Throwing Tantrums

Kevin and his son, Alex, were enjoying the community pool on a hot summer afternoon. After splashing around for several hours, Kevin told Alex that they'd be leaving in five minutes. When time was up, Kevin let Alex know it was time to get out of the pool. Alex refused, shouting that he wasn't leaving the pool. After several minutes of attempting to convince Alex to head onto dry land, Kevin waded back into the water, picked up his son who was now kicking and screaming, and dragged him over to their car.

You knew the toddler years would bring their fair share of tantrums, and you braced yourself for the chaos, but now that you've gotten past ages two and three you may be wondering if these meltdowns will ever end.

CAUSES

A tantrum is evidence of a brain that is having difficulty regulating emotions in a positive and productive way. In other words, something is bugging your kid, and everyone in a five-mile radius is going to hear about it. Even as adults, we experience moments like this, whether it's losing our cool when we're cut off in traffic or feeling overwhelmed by a big project at work. In these moments, our feelings are so intense we often can't respond in a calm, rational way. Regardless of age, we all benefit from being given the space and support to feel our own emotions.

Compared to toddlers, four-year-olds have greater cognitive abilities, language skills, and emotional awareness that may help minimize the frequency of tantrums, but they still struggle with self-regulation and need adult guidance to help them respond to situations in a calm way. For young children, tantrums are a way of communicating, and it is our responsibility to teach our children more effective ways of letting their needs be known. In Alex's case, he might have been tired or hungry, and that, plus finding out his fun was coming to an end, made a meltdown more likely.

PREVENTION

When you sense you're entering a situation in which your child might not happily follow your instructions, your first step is to remain calm. This can be extremely hard to do, but focus on connecting with your child before trying to get him to follow your instructions. Acknowledge his feelings by saying something like "You're mad because you wanted to keep swimming." Avoid saying things like "You're okay" or "Stop crying," as this tends to dismiss the very real emotions that your child is experiencing, and frankly, it isn't going to help your cause.

Another prevention tip: Learn to anticipate triggers. Are there certain times of day when your child is more prone to meltdowns? Could your child be hungry or tired? Pay attention to what tends to set him off and try to plan around it. For future pool trips, for example, it might be helpful if Kevin decided to leave the pool earlier, before Alex became overly tired and hungry.

IN THE MOMENT

Despite your best efforts, tantrums will likely still happen from time to time. When your child is mid-meltdown, let him express his feelings and then try to redirect him to a different activity. Avoid time-outs, as making your child sit on his own may make him feel abandoned when he's in need of connection and validation. Also, forget reasoning it out. When he's this upset, the odds of him saying "Oh, yes, I see your point" are exactly zero.

WHEN THE MOMENT HAS PASSED

Taming tantrums takes time, patience, and creativity to find what works best for your little one. Be consistent and give plenty of positive attention, praising the desired behaviors that you'd like to see continue. The next time Alex does something with minimal prompting, such as getting out of the pool the first time he's told, Kevin could comment, "Thank you for getting out so quickly when I said it was time to go home. I've had so much fun at the pool with you today."

Potty Problems

After having packed two sets of backup clothes for his daughter, Tim was surprised to see Nora walk out of her preschool classroom wearing a borrowed outfit. Nora had nearly two years of experience using the toilet, and Tim was getting increasingly frustrated by her frequent potty problems. By the age of four, most children have been using the toilet for some time, but it's not unusual for them to still struggle with accidents. Although these incidents generally subside over time, there are some things that you can do to help your child with this process.

CAUSES

If your child struggles with daytime wetting accidents, the reason could be simple: It's been too long since the last bathroom trip. Perhaps your child became engrossed in an activity and wasn't fully aware of the urge to go until it was too late. As children get older, they become more aware of their bladder and bowel cues and are less likely to experience these types of accidents. On the flip side, staying clean and dry at night is a developmental milestone that some children reach earlier than others, with some having accidents well into the school years.

PREVENTION

Check in with your child regularly to ask if she needs to use the restroom, or consider having scheduled times to go in and try. If there is a particular activity that seems to be associated with more accidents (like playing outside), then be sure to have your child attempt to go before heading out to play. On a practical note, always bring a change of clothes along when you go somewhere so you have a backup outfit for your child if needed.

If it's nighttime bed-wetting that your child struggles with, limit the amount of liquids your child consumes in the hour leading up to bedtime. Use a mattress protector to minimize the effects of accidents, and consider placing a small potty in the child's room for easy access. Most medical experts don't recommend treatment for nighttime wetting episodes until the child is six or seven years old.

IN THE MOMENT

When accidents occur, understand that they're not intentional; your child most likely didn't mean to soil his pants. Respond calmly and help your child change into a clean outfit, saying "I see that you've had an accident. Let's get some clean clothes on." Simple, to the point, and no worry about making your child feel bad.

WHEN THE MOMENT HAS PASSED

Toileting accidents are common for young children, especially within the first few years of potty training. For some, accidents may continue into the school-age years. Recognize that these accidents can be embarrassing for your child, especially if they occur in public places. Your child needs your love and understanding, as well as your guidance, as you explore possible solutions together.

Can't Sit Still

Recently I had one of those situations where all of my childcare options fell through and I had to bring my children along to my annual physical appointment. I could feel my blood pressure rising just thinking about how I'd get them to sit still long enough for me to get through my checkup. The only thing that could have been worse is if I'd had to take them to the DMV! Any parent who has to do that deserves a medal—and a couple rounds of drinks on the house.

CAUSES

As a general rule, I try to avoid situations like this at all costs, because it's simply not developmentally appropriate to expect young children to sit still for extended periods of time. It's not only that they *want* to be up and moving, they actually have a developmental need to be. That said, there will always be times when we have to bring children into situations that require sitting still. It could be trips to the doctor, air travel, religious services, or an older sibling's school concert that seems to stretch on for days.

PREVENTION

Build quiet times into your daily routine, giving your little one a chance to "practice" downtime. Calm activities can include reading books together, attending story time at your local library, sitting through family meals at the table, and even making time in your day for stretching, yoga, or mindfulness practices. All of these will give your child opportunities to practice self-control and sustained attention.

Also, be sure that your little one has plenty of active time as well. Get her outside, playing and enjoying the fresh air. The inability to sit still may sometimes stem from a lack of opportunity to get those muscles moving.

IN THE MOMENT

If you know that you'll need your child to sit still for a lengthy period of time, allow plenty of free movement beforehand to get some wiggles out. This could mean

walking your child around the airline terminal before board-
ing a plane or riding bikes outside before heading out on a
long car trip.

Most importantly, bring activities with you to keep your
child occupied during the appointment or trip. I like to
fill a small bag with stickers, crayons, notepads, stamps,
mini containers of clay, bubbles, and other entertaining
items. Also, snacks. Lots of snacks. In our everyday routine,
we have relatively set snack times, but on these "special
occasions" I bring many snacks, which help keep my kids
occupied and content.

WHEN THE MOMENT HAS PASSED

After barely surviving my doctor's visit with my little ones
in tow, I was feeling on edge, so I took the kids to our neighborhood splash pad for a couple of hours. At other times,
we'll follow a period of having to be still with a wiggle-fest,
when we run and dance to our hearts' content. My point is,
try to reward the "stay still" time with some opportunities to
move. Finally, I know it can be nerve-racking to keep your
child's behavior in check, but try not to stress too much. It
will get easier as your child gets older and gains the physical, cognitive, and social/emotional abilities to sit still for
longer periods of time. That said, if your child continues
to have difficulty with this task into later years or shows
greater difficulty than most children, speak with a medical
professional and consider screenings for ADHD (attention deficit hyperactivity disorder) or sensory processing
disorder.

A MOMENT OF SANITY

Four-year-olds are often a mix of intense emotions, curiosity, and energy. It's normal to become overwhelmed by the demands and liveliness of your child at this age. Don't be surprised if you find yourself drained from the number of questions your child asks in a day. Seriously, so many questions. Do yourself a favor: After a particularly long day, hop into the tub and soak up the fact that no one is commenting on your pimples or dirty teeth.

5 YEAR OLDS

Centers of the Universe

FRIENDS SARAH AND RANI were sitting together coloring pictures of rainbows and chatting about their upcoming birthday parties. An argument erupted over whose turn it was to use the blue crayon, and Rani refused to fork over the coveted color. Sarah stood up and angrily shouted, "Then you can't come to my birthday party!" If I had a dollar for every time I heard this when I was teaching little ones, I'd probably be retired right now, lounging on a beach somewhere in the Caribbean.

What's New

At age five, children have a growing interest in friendships and a desire to be accepted by their peers. At the same time, they continue to struggle with egocentrism, which makes seeing another's perspective challenging. They are still learning effective conflict resolution skills and are slowly developing their ability to regulate emotions in a productive and prosocial way. Consistent modeling of appropriate actions is the best approach to combating undesirable behaviors.

Five-year-olds have an improving ability to follow directions, which is especially beneficial as most enter kindergarten around this age. They also have a greater ability to discern the difference between fantasy and reality. In addition, they're beginning to develop an idea of what's right and what's wrong, although their understanding tends to remain very simple and rule oriented for some time.

Some of the physical development milestones children experience in year five include using the toilet without assistance, writing their own name, and learning to tie shoes. You may notice that your little one is also looking longer and leaner, leaving the typical chubbiness of toddlerhood behind.

Capabilities and Limitations

At this age, children are aware of gender and have created schemas, or a way of organizing information, about what is male and what is female. These schemas are often stereotyped and heavily influenced by the adults with whom the children regularly interact.

Five-year-olds have improving memories and can retell events that have happened while using the appropriate tense. They will often ask the meaning of new words and may even begin to recognize commonly seen words in books. They're speaking in more complete and complex sentences and have a greater understanding of concept words like *bigger, taller, smallest*, and so on. Additionally, they're able to use present, past, and future tenses conversationally. Reading together is recommended, as it helps boost vocabulary, increases their repertoire of sight words, and provides opportunities for special one-on-one time with parents.

Communication

When it comes to talking with kids, I like to go back to '90s pop music for a catchy reminder of a very important communication rule for parents: Tell me what you want, what you really, really want. In other words, be very clear with your child about what behavior you'd like to see, and keep the statements about what you *don't* want to see to a minimum. For instance, if your child is throwing sand at other children, before the words "stop," "no," or "don't" come out of your mouth, consider the behavior that you actually would like to see. With that in mind, you might respond with "Put the sand in your bucket" or "Scoop the sand with your shovel." This helps to redirect an undesirable behavior—blinding the other kids with sand—to one that is more appropriate, like making a sandcastle. Your "do" statements let your child know very specifically what you expect of him.

DISCIPLINE

One facet of discipline is helping our kids figure out how to manage their emotions in appropriate and healthy ways. Although we want to respect kids' rights to their feelings, we also want to help them find successful ways to manage their emotions, whether it's through drawing pictures, going for a walk, or taking deep breaths. In some instances, a silly dance might be just the way to defuse a situation or mitigate an impending meltdown. If you sense a tantrum brewing, consider saying, "I'm starting to feel a little upset (amped up, tense—take your pick). I'm going to do some silly dancing to help me feel better. Want to do it with me?" Shake your booty, jump up and down, swing your arms around, and be as silly as possible. This often captures children's attention and redirects their behavior to something more productive—in this case, boogying instead of freaking out.

Why does this work? Movement and rhythmic activity have been shown to increase regulatory abilities and bring the brain back to a state in which it's more capable of responding instead of reacting. If you've ever gone on a walk or run, worked out, or done yoga or another physical activity as a means of lowering stress and boosting your mood, you've done the same thing for your brain. To quote Elle Woods in *Legally Blonde*, "Exercise gives you endorphins. Endorphins make you happy." And if all else fails, you could always try to crack your kid up with your version of Elle's famous "bend and snap"!

COMMON CONUNDRUMS

Getting Dressed Drama

The hour or more it took Jada to get dressed for school each morning was getting her family's day off to a lousy start. By the time she was finally ready, Jada usually had to skip breakfast and head straight to the car with red and puffy eyes from a morning filled with tears. Her mom became increasingly frustrated trying to get Jada and her siblings out the door and to school on time. Perhaps you can relate to this cycle, where you wake up dreading the struggle that you know awaits you.

CAUSES
Wanting to have a say in their clothing choice is a normal part of development in children at this age. Though we want to provide kids with opportunities to demonstrate their growing independence, we also want to get to school

and work on time with our sanity at least somewhat intact. Striking a balance between allowing children freedom and enforcing the limits we've set can sometimes be confusing and stressful. Yelling, scolding, punishing, and bargaining with kids typically leads us further into a power struggle and doesn't get us any closer to leaving the house on time.

PREVENTION

Take an inventory of your child's wardrobe. Is the closet jam-packed and are the dresser drawers stuffed so tightly that it's impossible to see what's in there? If so, go full-on Marie Kondo and ditch anything that's too small, too stained, or never worn. Clothes that are too large or out of season should be stored out of sight. (Think top of the closet or in bins under the bed.) If, after purging and storing, there are still many pieces to choose from, try picking your child's favorite items and packing others away for a while. Simply having fewer choices should help your child select an outfit more swiftly.

IN THE MOMENT

Move the outfit selection process from the already-frantic a.m. to the hopefully calmer evening before. You may even find that selecting a week's worth of outfits on Sunday can set you up for a less stressful week. A fun tip: Snap photos of your child in some of her favorite outfits so she has ideas to work from.

If, after all that, you still find yourself in a battle over getting dressed in the morning, it may be time to allow for natural consequences. In this case, you could tell your child that you'll be leaving at 7:30 a.m. regardless of whether she's ready or not. You'll have an outfit for her in the car, or she may choose to get ready before then. If she's not ready when it's time to go, everyone gets in the car, pajamas and all. A natural consequence, in this case, would mean that she goes to school in her pajamas, though she has the choice to change in the car before getting out. Either way, you're not letting your morning be derailed by a tiny tyrant who insists on wearing a stained T-shirt and high-waters.

WHEN THE MOMENT HAS PASSED

Later in the day, check in with your child about the morning clothing struggle: "You seemed to have a really hard time getting dressed this morning. What could we do differently tomorrow to help us get out the door on time?" Get your child involved in the problem-solving process by asking him for ideas on how to make getting dressed go more smoothly in the future.

On a final note, some children may have difficulty with sensory experiences. If you find that your child is very particular about certain sensations or articles of clothing, stick to ones that work for him. If the issue is very persistent, consider having your child screened for sensory processing disorder, a condition in which the brain has a difficult time receiving and processing information when overwhelmed by external stimuli.

Separation Anxiety

It was Teddy's first day of kindergarten, and his mom had planned every detail of the morning to celebrate this momentous occasion. There was a new first-day-of-school outfit, a special pancake breakfast, and of course, a mini photo shoot out front before heading to school. Nerves were high for both Teddy and his mom as they embarked on this new and exciting chapter in their lives. As they walked up to the classroom, Teddy suddenly went into hysterics, crying and clinging to his mother's leg.

CAUSES

Although separation anxiety often begins in infancy and can extend well into the school years, I thought it would be helpful to discuss it in this chapter, as many children experience some nervousness when starting kindergarten. For some, it's their first regular, prolonged time away from home and parents, whereas others may already have experience in preschool or another childcare setting. Regardless, it's not uncommon for children to display anxiety, and perhaps even have some behavioral issues because of this uneasiness. Starting "real school" is a big step and can be overwhelming for both kids and parents.

PREVENTION

When it's time for your child to start kindergarten (or any new school), consider downplaying the significance of the day. This might sound crazy in the Instagram age, when we're used to the fanfare of personalized chalkboards and photo shoots worthy of a fashion magazine, but creating a lot of commotion around the event can cause extra stress for your little one. If you can, visit the school before the first day to give your child time to get acquainted with the new surroundings. Once school starts, have your child take along a transitional object, one that may offer comfort, like a stuffed animal or a favorite book. Leave a note, drawing, or photo in your child's lunchbox to offer love and support midday.

IN THE MOMENT

Create a *quick* goodbye ritual such as a hug and kiss or a high-five. Don't linger; just do your routine, say goodbye, and get going. As a former educator, I know that a quick goodbye is better for all involved. As a parent, I also fully understand the angst over leaving your child. Talk with the teacher about checking in after a certain amount of time to see how your child is doing. If your child is upset when you leave, know that he will most likely calm down within a few minutes. Finally, be specific with your child about when you'll be back, and follow through: "I'll be back after lunch time" or "When I'm done with work, I'll come pick you up. It will be after your snack time this afternoon."

WHEN THE MOMENT HAS PASSED
Use books to help your child cope with this transition. Some of my favorites include *The Kissing Hand* by Audrey Penn, *Wemberly Worried* by Kevin Henkes, and *Llama Llama Misses Mama* by Anna Dewdney. In our house, we're also big fans of the *Daniel Tiger's Neighborhood* episode featuring the theme "Grown-Ups Come Back." These help children navigate the anxiety of leaving parents and going to new places through fun and relatable stories.

Picky Eaters

Given my educational background and experience working with young children, I entered into parenting with a pretty big ego surrounding kids and food. That didn't last long. As my daughter got older, she became much more particular about foods that she liked and disliked, and these preferences seemed to change by the hour. She became increasingly skeptical of vegetables and anything even remotely green, and she went through phases where she insisted on living off yogurt and grilled cheese.

Perhaps you're living with a child who requests mac and cheese for breakfast, lunch, and dinner. Maybe you're exhausted from the daily battle of trying to get a single vegetable into your child's stomach. Last week I overheard a group of moms talking about their children's eating habits, and one exasperated mom said, "I just don't get it! I mean, she likes cheese and she likes tortillas, but she doesn't like quesadillas?! It's just the two put together, kid!" Sigh, at least we're not alone.

CAUSES

Fussing over food is very common for children and usually not something to be concerned about. It's normal for them to go through food fads, where they insist on eating the same meal over and over. As little ones move through their preschool and school-age years, they may reject foods as a way of asserting their developing autonomy and independence.

PREVENTION

Ellyn Satter, a registered dietician and family therapist, is well-known for her approach to feeding children. In her book *Child of Mine: Feeding with Love and Good Sense*, she argues that parents are responsible for selecting and preparing foods, providing regular meals and snacks, creating a pleasant eating environment, and modeling positive mealtime behaviors. Children? They're mainly tasked with eating until their hunger cues are satisfied. The beauty of utilizing this approach is that it eliminates the food power struggle (i.e., the seventh circle of parenting hell), and it doesn't turn us into short order cooks trying to please every palate.

When you're outside of your usual routine, like Thanksgiving dinner at Grandma's house, you can still use this division of responsibility. Prepare your child's plate with small portions of a variety of foods, like mashed potatoes, green bean casserole, turkey, and cranberries. Your child has the choice to eat whatever is on his plate. If he doesn't want to touch Aunt Linda's green bean casserole (and honestly, who can blame him?), then let it sit on the plate. Regardless of the setting, his responsibility is to eat until his hunger cues are satisfied.

IN THE MOMENT

When preparing your child's plate, offer less food than you think she'll eat. We tend to overfill our children's plates, and the amount of food may be overwhelming and, ultimately, a turn off to young eaters. Your child can always ask for more if needed. Also, consider the way you present foods, especially those that kids may be less than excited to encounter. I'm in no way suggesting that you should turn out color-coordinated, Pinterest-worthy meals, but if serving carrots shredded instead of in larger pieces or cutting a PB&J sandwich with a circle cookie cutter isn't too much of a pain, it may be worth it. Also, if you've got one of those kids who loathes his food touching, try putting foods on divided plates or in muffin tins or ice cube trays to keep everything separate.

Finally, don't underestimate the power of offering foods with a simple dip like yogurt, salsa, hummus, or ketchup. I've found my kids will eat pretty much anything they can dip. I've even witnessed one dipping orange slices in ranch dressing. Kind of gross, yes, but I'm still considering it a win.

WHEN THE MOMENT HAS PASSED

Stay the course of offering a variety of healthy, nutritious options, and don't get too hung up on the day-to-day oddities of kids' food choices. You can't control what your child puts in his mouth, but you do get to decide what foods he's exposed to. Take your child along on your next shopping trip, and encourage him to pick out a new veggie to try from the produce aisle. You've probably heard this before, but it really is true: When children are involved in shopping for and preparing food, they are much more inclined to at least give it a try.

Bedtime Battles

You've been there; I know you have. It's approaching bedtime, the finish line is in sight, and the anticipation of a few hours of child-free time is palpable. You might even be envisioning what you'll do with those coveted nighttime hours. Fold the eight loads of laundry on the floor? Wash the dishes in the sink? Watch half an episode of the latest Netflix series before passing out on the couch?

But, alas, the requests keep rolling in: another glass of water, several trips to the bathroom, two more bedtime stories. Many tears—usually yours—and what feels like 10 years later, your child is finally asleep. Meanwhile, you're so exhausted that Netflix is out of the question and you'll be lucky to keep your eyes open long enough to brush your teeth before bed.

CAUSES

Young children are wired to test and push boundaries, which means that they often rage against the routine. In some instances, they may be overtired and therefore more susceptible to meltdowns, or they may not be tired yet and turn to protestations in order to stay up a bit longer. It's important to take a look at your current bedtime routine, as well as the developmental needs of your child. With these in mind, you can find an approach that is appropriate and predictable for your child—and less exhausting for you.

PREVENTION

Establishing a consistent routine is critical for young children, especially at bedtime, because it gives them a heads-up about what's coming next. In our house, our evening routine begins with family dinner. After this, it's bath and pajamas for the kids. We then have playtime together, usually doing "wind-down" activities such as coloring, reading, or playing with puppets. If weather permits, we like to go on an evening walk around the neighborhood. Once we're approaching bedtime, we brush teeth, snuggle, share our favorite parts of the day, and give goodnight hugs and kisses. The kids are allowed to look at books in bed until they fall asleep.

IN THE MOMENT

Allow sufficient wind-down time during which your child engages in calm activities. If necessary, bump up the start time of your evening routine to make time for this. It may be helpful to eliminate screen time in the hours leading up to bed. Read books, color, or even try some basic yoga poses alongside your child.

If your kid is feeling a lack of say in the routine, it may help if you give him options: "Would you like to wear the red pajamas or the blue ones?" "Would you like two night-time stories or three?" When children feel like they have no input in decisions that affect them, they tend to rebel, which makes bedtime tougher on everyone.

WHEN THE MOMENT HAS PASSED

Bedtime battles are typically not won overnight (pun intended). Consistency is key, even if this means leading your child back to his room for the tenth time. In the morning, once everyone is a bit more rested and levelheaded, remind your child that he's loved no matter what, but that getting enough rest is important for staying healthy. Find times to give him undivided attention during the day, and when evening comes, jump right back into your routine.

Fears

At a routine visit to the doctor, Brooke learned that she'd be getting a shot. Once she heard the news, she burst into tears in the exam room. Her dad tried reasoning with her that it would only take a second and then it would be over, but it didn't help. She became louder and louder as she went into full hysterics. Becoming increasingly angry at this outburst, her dad insisted that she stop crying, commenting that she was behaving ridiculously. This only served to fan the flames of her meltdown.

Whether it's fear of an injection or monsters lurking under the bed, most kids have at least one or two things that make them especially skittish. Oftentimes, parents feel confused and helpless about their child's seemingly irrational fears and the outbursts that they bring.

CAUSES

Fears are very common throughout childhood and may occur for a variety of reasons, ranging from negative experiences to seeing something scary on television. Overall, fear is a good thing because it helps us to be cautious and look out for potentially dangerous situations. When a fear inhibits the ability to function in everyday life, then it becomes a problem. As children grow, their fears may shift according to their developmental abilities. Babies and toddlers fear separation from their parents, as well as new and unfamiliar faces or situations. Preschoolers tend to fear the dark and monsters under their bed. School-age children may fear real-life dangers such as natural disasters or "bad guys."

PREVENTION

Though it's not possible or beneficial to prevent your child from ever experiencing fear, it can be helpful to prepare her ahead of time if a fearful situation is coming up. For example, letting Brooke know that she'd be receiving a shot at the doctor's office beforehand could have given her a chance to experience the intensity of her emotions at home, allowing her dad to talk with her about the fear prior to sitting in the exam room.

For the all-too-common fear of the dark, I suggest trying some "in the dark" activities besides bedtime. Turn the lights off in the evening and use glow sticks or a black light. Go outside and play flashlight tag. Don't let bedtime be your child's only encounter with the dark. It may also be beneficial to use night-lights in your child's room for bedtime so that there is still some visibility. Also, avoid television shows that are scary or have dark themes, as children may interpret that information as happening to them or directly near them.

IN THE MOMENT

Be attentive to your child's concern, and reflect back what's worrying her: "You're feeling scared about getting a shot. It's okay to be afraid" or "When it's dark, you can't see anything and you're afraid there might be something scary in your room." Once you've acknowledged the concern, you can use some practical steps to help your child calm down: "Would it help if I held your hand while the doctor is here?" "Would it help if we put a night-light in your bedroom?"

WHEN THE MOMENT HAS PASSED

It may be beneficial to spend some time addressing stress in your child's life. Is there anything new going on? New school? A move to a new home? New sibling? Big events in a child's life may cause anxiety that may manifest as new fears. With love, patience, and reassurance, these fears tend to diminish over time. If there has been any trauma in the child's life, seek medical advice and reach out to mental health professionals.

A MOMENT OF SANITY

With their increasing independence and slowly improving emotional skills, five-year-olds may seem mature one day but can still be explosive and erratic the next. Riding these waves can often be stressful, so when the waters get especially choppy, reach out to some friends or family members who can throw you a life raft. Even a quick phone call or text message can remind you that you're not alone. Better still, an evening out with your partner or friends can be a great way to recharge. You've got this!

6 YEAR OLDS

Rule Enforcers

A FEW WEEKS BACK, my kids and I took a trip to a local amusement park. As we entered the dinosaur excavation exhibit—essentially a large sandbox filled with tools and imitation fossils—a girl playing nearby jumped up and shouted, "Excuse me, lady! You guys can't wear shoes in here!" We thanked her for letting us know, took off our shoes, and continued on our way. A moment later, she popped up again and stated emphatically, "No, you need to go put your shoes up there where they belong." Her mom approached me and apologized for her daughter's insistence on abiding by the shoe policy. I assured her it was no problem, then silently thanked them for this perfect illustration of the classic six-year-olds' love of laws.

What's New

At this age, kids understand that there are rules to be followed, and they often rigidly expect others to fall in line—and they're not shy about calling out anyone who doesn't. Some developmentalists consider this a coping strategy that helps children feel more secure in a world that can seem unpredictable and scary. Regardless of the reason, spend any time around children of this age, and you're likely to hear some protest surrounding others' rule breaking.

As kids leave the early childhood stage and forge forward into the exciting years of middle childhood, they experience many developmental changes, including increasing cognitive abilities. Children are beginning to process information in more advanced ways, which allows them to bring more order to a sometimes-chaotic world. One example of this mental progression is the ability to sort objects based on characteristics such as size, shape, or color. This process, known as seriation, allows children to categorize a wide range of items, an ability that can help them as they learn about the world around them.

Capabilities and Limitations

During this time, children usually develop the ability to understand that the amount of something stays the same even when its appearance changes. For instance, if a ball of dough is rolled out and twisted into a rope, the rope has the same amount of dough as the ball. Likewise, a cup of liquid looks different in a tall, skinny glass than it does in a short, wider one.

Six-year-olds have improving hand-eye coordination, which can help them in school, during play, and in activities of daily living. They're interested in mastering their skills and enjoy showing off their newfound talents. A strong desire to be first or best emerges, and competition begins to reign in the lives of these young ones. If you've ever seen the no-holds-barred race to be line leader, then you're already familiar with this phenomenon.

It's not uncommon for children to develop best friends and enemies at this age, as their peer group takes on a more important role. Children have a strong desire to be included in friend groups, and they begin to dread being excluded.

Communication

Have you ever tried to have a conversation with someone while you're sitting on the ground and they're standing? It's awkward and not all that conducive to meaningful conversation. Since most adults tower over kids, when talking with them, it's important to get down to their level and show that you're engaged in the conversation through eye contact and active listening. Sit with your child and allow him to lead your time together, whether this involves building with blocks or acting out a superhero story. As you're interacting, you have a great opportunity to ask questions about his day.

Some children, particularly those who are on the autism spectrum, have difficulty making eye contact. Eye contact should not be forced or demanded, but you can still get down to their level to better engage them in conversation.

One of the biggest goals of parenting is to provide children with the tools and skills needed for self-regulation, which allows children to feel their emotions without having those emotions dictate reactions or behaviors. As parents, we can use daily interactions and struggles to help children understand their behaviors and increase their ability to respond appropriately in challenging situations. Although innate temperament certainly plays a role in how your child reacts (we covered this in depth on page 5), you have a profound impact on her learned responses. When you model calm composure in the heat of the moment, you help train your child's brain to do the same. Over time, a calm and clear-headed response becomes the default in stressful situations.

Here's an analogy to illustrate the process. About a year ago, I began mountain biking with my husband. As a novice, I prefer trails that are heavily traveled because they are free from major obstacles and overgrown brush. The path is easier and quicker to navigate because it has been used over and over. The more I ride these trails, the more second-nature riding becomes. By contrast, forging a new trail takes significantly more time and energy.

In a very simplified way, our brains operate similarly: The more we do something a certain way, the more second-nature it becomes. If your emotions tend to escalate quickly and you struggle most days with keeping your cool, you've likely unintentionally trained your brain to go down that path. The good news is that it's possible—with time, effort, and desire—to forge a new path, and you can teach your child to do the same.

Hurt Feelings

Amy came home from school in tears because her friends informed her that she could no longer be part of their group. Her mom, Cindy, fought the urge to call the parents of the other girls and scold them for the way their kids treated her daughter. As parents, it's natural to want to swoop in and make all the hard things in our children's lives disappear. And we used to be able to do that. Just a few years ago, when your toddler scraped her knee, all it took was a gentle kiss to make the hurt disappear. Now that she's getting older, the wounds are becoming more complex. In this case, Cindy knew she couldn't fix the situation or stop her daughter's pain by confronting the other moms. Instead, she needed to be supportive of her daughter's feelings and help her manage her intense emotions so she could learn healthy ways of navigating tough situations.

CAUSES

As much as we hate it, our kids will have their feelings hurt a hundred times over throughout their lives. For humans with complex, emotional brains, this is the cost of doing business. Help your child differentiate between feelings and behaviors. Feelings are neither good nor bad, right nor wrong. You can feel however you want. Behaviors, on the other hand, have consequences. There are behaviors that are appropriate and acceptable, as well as ones that are not.

PREVENTION
Our job as parents is not to prevent our children from feeling pain. Rather, our job is to give them the tools to survive heartbreak. It's healthy for children to experience a range of emotions, to learn how to sit with them and navigate the ups and downs of life. This is part of being human, and it is a valuable skill to learn, as hard things will challenge us throughout our entire lives.

IN THE MOMENT
When your child comes to you with hurt feelings, remain calm and avoid jumping in with a plan to "fix" the problem. Give your child a safe place to struggle with the feelings. Your role is to be a supportive listener. This is a great opportunity for you to practice active listening and ask reflective questions: "How did it feel when they said those things?" "Why do you think they might have said that?" "What could you do in the future if you find yourself in a similar situation?" Demonstrate care and empathy for your child, and encourage your child to consider other children's perspectives.

WHEN THE MOMENT HAS PASSED
Think about what the response was when you experienced difficult feelings as a child. Were you told to buck up? Taken out for ice cream to distract you from hurt feelings? Were you ignored? Listened to? Those responses may

impact how you now respond to your own child. Avoid any approach that serves to jump in and fix the situation, as it may temporarily provide a distraction from the discomfort but ultimately sacrifices an opportunity for your child to develop healthy resilience. Focus on being a source of support and strength for your child by reminding her that it's okay to feel hurt and sad, that these feelings come and go throughout life, and that they won't last forever.

Though you may want to tell off the child who hurt your child, understand that kids are navigating the complex world of friendships, and this means that they'll do things that hurt others. Though hurt feelings are common in childhood and, when handled appropriately, can provide opportunities for emotional growth, it's important to note that bullying should be addressed by you and the adults involved in the setting in which it took place (e.g., school, a friend's home). We'll talk more about bullying on page 147.

Swear Words

The only time I ever consider bringing a dog into our family is when I'm crouched under our dining table cleaning up the food remnants from our most recent meal. After cleaning up the mess recently, I stood up too quickly and hit my head on the edge of the table. Before I could stop myself, "Ugh, dammit!" came out of my mouth. I quickly whispered a prayer that neither of my children had heard me. No one repeated the word, so I seemed to be in the clear. Fast forward a few days to Easter when we gathered with our extended family. When my daughter dropped one of her egg hunt treasures, she loudly proclaimed, "Oh dammit!"

I immediately sank down into my chair, crossing every finger and toe that no one—especially my mother-in-law—had heard.

CAUSES

Sometimes (okay, maybe often) we are the culprits when it comes to naughty words. If not you, then it could be a spouse, relative, neighbor, or friend. Other times, it might be from a television show, movie, or video game. Unfortunately, it's difficult, if not impossible, to completely shield children from hearing undesirable words.

PREVENTION

Obviously, the best way to prevent cussing is to limit your child's exposure to profanity. Select television shows and movies that are age appropriate, be aware of the songs that you play in the car, and work on taming your own tongue. Even with all that, my guess is that at some point, your child will still pick up a naughty word.

Sometimes, use of the word is a novelty, and your child will say it for fun and to gain attention. In other cases, it may be used out of frustration or anger. If the latter is the case, work on finding more positive and socially acceptable ways of managing emotions, for yourself and for your child.

IN THE MOMENT

Drawing excessive attention to a forbidden word makes it much more exciting and interesting to kids, so stay calm and don't make a big deal out of it. If the word continues to come up, try offering your child a more suitable alternative. In this case, if my daughter says "dammit," I reply with "Oh, shoot!" or "Bummer!"

If swearing is a persistent issue, especially among many members of your family, consider instituting a no-swearing rule and adding a consequence. This could involve paying a quarter to the swear jar or losing a privilege. The important thing is that everyone, including you, is held accountable to the rule.

After the fact, it may be helpful to give a calm explanation about why the word is inappropriate. You could say something like, "That's not a nice word to use. Let's use _____ instead." If you know you've said this word in the past, you might even add, "I'm sorry for saying that before. I shouldn't have done that." Let your little one know that it is an adult word, one that she can choose to use when she's an adult. You can liken it to adult movies, shows, drinks, and so on that you have to be older to choose.

Body Exploration

Dylan and his family had settled down to watch a movie together. When his mom glanced over at him, she noticed that Dylan had his hand down his pants and appeared to be playing with his penis. For many parents, the immediate reaction would be to say, "Hey! Get your hand out of there!" Exploring their body, including the genital area, is part of typical child development and should be expected. So, what are parents to do when they look over and see their kid doing some private investigating?

CAUSES

From about 18 months of age, toddlers begin to explore their genitals. Quite simply, they are curious about their bodies, and it feels good to touch down there. This self-exploration is actually a healthy part of development for both girls and boys. However, parents are often caught off guard because we don't tend to think about sexuality in regard to children.

PREVENTION

The conversation about sexuality is one that takes place little by little over time. It's important to communicate to your child that touching oneself is natural, but there are certain places where it's not appropriate. Consider it this way: Screaming and yelling aren't necessarily bad, but there are places, say a religious service or the doctor's office, where these actions are not socially acceptable. Likewise, touching one's body isn't inherently bad; we just want to help children understand the appropriate context for it. Your child's bedroom or the bathroom may be an acceptable place, whereas shared family spaces or public areas are not. Avoid forbidding children to touch themselves. Doing so sets them up to view this as shameful and taboo, something that will then only be done in secrecy and with unnecessary guilt.

IN THE MOMENT

Use accurate and anatomically correct terminology when speaking with your child: "Please don't touch your vulva/penis right now." You might also consider letting your child know of a more acceptable time and place: "We're having family time right now, which is not an appropriate time for touching your vulva/penis." Without imposing any shame, you're establishing clear boundaries for the behavior.

Once you've laid the groundwork with accurate terminology and have explained appropriate times and settings, you can add other ways of addressing the issue. Try ignoring the action and redirecting to a different activity. In Dylan's case, his mom might say, "Oh, we forgot snacks! Dylan, come in the kitchen and help me get the popcorn." In other instances, parents might try something like, "I was thinking it might be fun to paint right now. Do you want to do that together?" or "Let's go outside and take a walk while it's still sunny out." The goal is to get your child engaged in a different activity without drawing undue attention to the undesired behavior. This tactic is especially helpful if you're with other people and you want to stop the behavior without embarrassing your child.

WHEN THE MOMENT HAS PASSED

Once Dylan and his mom are in the kitchen, she could gently remind him about the proper times and places for touching: "When we were in the other room, I noticed you were touching your penis. Remember that the family room is not an appropriate place for that."

A very important piece of the ongoing sexuality dialogue is safety with others. Let your child know that although it's okay to explore his own body, it's never okay for others to touch his genitals. Remind him that it's important for him to tell you if anyone touches him or asks to see private areas.

On a final note, if genital exploration and stimulation occurs frequently, cannot be redirected, causes emotional or physical pain, mimics adult sexual acts, or involves coercion, seek medical advice, as these may be signs of developmental difficulties or sexual abuse.

Whining

If we were ever going to use the "nails on a chalkboard" analogy, it would be here. Whining can take any relatively calm, clear-headed parent and launch him or her over the edge into complete madness. Maybe you've been in a situation like this: You're driving home and your child asks for a snack, only you don't have any snacks with you (which is the worst. Never leave the house without snacks). Not getting her requested snack, she begins to whine louder and louder, and you think to yourself, "Why on earth can't you just wait quietly, child?!" You may even find your own volume increasing as you try to reason with her that she'll get a snack as soon as you get home.

CAUSES

Kids aren't adults, and they're still learning how to appropriately make requests, respond to frustrating situations, and communicate in socially appropriate ways. Also, children want (and need) your attention, and quite frankly, whining is a very effective way of getting it.

PREVENTION

Make a habit of commenting on the behaviors that you want to see in your child. For example, you might tell your child, "I love the way you asked for more strawberries!" when she asks politely. This shows appreciation for positive behaviors and clues in your child to appropriate ways to request things—which makes her more likely to speak nicely in the future. So instead of repeating "Stop whining!" ad nauseam, when you catch your child *not* whining, pile on the praise.

IN THE MOMENT

Confronting whining with logic rarely works and often amps up the irritating behavior. Instead, say something like, "Oh, you're hungry! I'm so hungry, too! I wish we had snacks right now." Or "If I could have any snack, I'd pick cheese and apples. What would you pick? Let's think about what snack we'll make when we get home." Also, let your child know that you're having a hard time understanding him because of the way he's asking. Explain that when people speak clearly and don't whine, it's much easier to understand them.

Though it may be tempting to ignore whining, especially when it persists, I caution you to avoid this approach. Whining may not be our preferred mode of communication, but it's a mode your child uses to try to tell you something. Disregarding it may send the message that your child's needs don't matter. Our goal as parents is to promote connection, and ignoring a call for attention may work against this aim.

WHEN THE MOMENT HAS PASSED

Whining may not disappear overnight, but hang in there. Focus on approaching it with a loving and playful attitude, and remind yourself that your ultimate goal is connection with your child. Understand that whining is a form of communication, and help your child learn more effective ways to express her needs and desires. Headphones can help, too— just kidding!

Defiance

After three hours and countless reminders to clean up his room, Cody still hadn't picked up a single item. Seeing that nothing had been done, his mom reminded him yet again that he needed to get things tidied up, to which he responded emphatically, "No! You can't make me. You're not the boss of me!" Even the most chill parent is likely to snap back with an angry "In fact, I *am* the boss of you! Clean your room now!" If you're like me, then you've had moments like these when your child's continued defiance agitated you to your core and you got into a can't-win power struggle. I hate to say it, but we invite this type of battle when we shift into angry control mode and try to force our children to do what we want. In the short term, it sometimes leads to your child doing what you said. However, it fails in the long term because we lose out on a valuable opportunity for connection through calm limit setting.

CAUSES

At times, your child's defiance may take the form of angry back talk (more on this on page 142), whereas other times it might involve dawdling, dragging feet, or ignoring requests. Children may tune you out or act defiantly for a variety of reasons. It could come from a feeling of powerlessness ("I have no say in anything"), disinterest in the requested activity, being distracted by something more exciting, or even just good old-fashioned boundary pushing—all of which are to be expected. Throughout many ages and stages, children have the important task of testing limits and adult guidelines as they become increasingly independent and assertive and learn how to have some control over their own world.

PREVENTION

Reinforce positive behaviors by commenting on them when you see them: "Wow! I love how you cleaned your room. It looks great!" or "I'm proud of you for putting your plate in the sink without even being asked." Give your child opportunities to assert his independence and have some control over his own choices: "Would you rather clean your room before lunch or after lunch?" "Would you like me to help clean your room or would you like to do it by yourself?" Make your expectations very clear, and pick your battles. A clean room might not be something you're willing to compromise on, but perhaps you can let your kid slide on wearing a jacket outside, provided it's safe to do so.

IN THE MOMENT

You're probably still wondering what to do when your child flat-out refuses to listen. First and foremost, find a way to get yourself back to a calm place, because these moments can make any parent feel angry. When I find myself going into angry boss mode, I remind myself that my child's behavior—though intensely irritating—is developmentally expected, and that she's counting on me to teach her how to respond more appropriately. Once you're calm enough to continue, remind your child of your expectations while also acknowledging how she's feeling. For instance, you might reply, "Wow. You must be very upset. We don't talk to each other (or act) that way, and I think you know that." After addressing the defiance, you can move forward into finding solutions: "I expect you to clean your room. Would you rather pick up your toys or your clothes first?"

In some cases, connecting what you want done to a fun activity or privilege may be helpful. For instance, telling your child that he won't be allowed to watch a TV show until his room has been cleaned or that she can't play outside unless her jacket is on can motivate your child to follow through with the expected behavior.

WHEN THE MOMENT HAS PASSED

Later on, touch base with your child about the episode. Referring back to the earlier example, Cody's mom might have a chat with him during the bedtime routine: "It took you a long time to clean your room today, and you seemed pretty angry when I came to check on you. What do you think would help you next time when your room needs to be cleaned?"

More often than not, periods of defiance come and go throughout childhood. For more tips on winning the chore wars, check out page 100. However, if you're concerned about the frequency and intensity of your child's defiant behaviors, seek medical advice. Some children meet the criteria for oppositional defiant disorder, and with this diagnosis, the approach will likely include different strategies and interventions.

A MOMENT OF SANITY

Even parents with the patience of saints are likely to lose it on days that are rife with whining and defiance. When your ears are on the verge of bleeding from your kid's incessant complaints, turn on your favorite '90s boy band (or whatever takes you back to a less stressful time, if the Backstreet Boys aren't your jam). Crank up the volume, and dance like no one is watching.

Rotating Hobbyists

JUAN AND HIS MOM were at a stalemate over his Halloween costume. He wanted scary and gory; she preferred light and fun. They finally agreed upon a clown costume, and that's where Juan's fascination with comic performers started. Over the next few months, Juan and his mom went to the circus and community festivals to see clowns. When Juan saw one making balloon animals at a local event, he was fascinated. Ultimately, Juan enrolled in Clown School and went to weekly classes for three months, learning the tricks of the trade, such as face painting, crafting balloon animals, and performing magic tricks. As a graduate of the program, he had a blast participating in parades, performing at retirement parties and entertaining at church events as "Kris the Krazy Clown."

I love this story because it's an unusual and comical hobby for a child. More importantly, it highlights the innate curiosity that children have, and how around this age, they often begin to form near-obsessions with their interests— assuming they have support for them. For some children, it's horseback riding or skateboarding. For others, it may be soccer, ballet, or painting. For Juan, aka Kris the Krazy Clown, it's clowning around.

DEVELOPMENT

What's New

Seven-year-olds tend to rely heavily on routines, much like they did in their early childhood years. They like predict-ability and rhythm to their days, although they're getting better at handling transitions and last-minute changes. Having lost the egocentrism of their younger years, they now consider others' feelings and opinions more, which can sometimes lead to their own hurt feelings and susceptibil-ity to peer pressure. Embarrassment or losing a game may feel crushing to their self-esteem. They have an increasing desire to be part of their friend groups. Though they do begin to care more about spending time with peers, they also show an increased interest in alone time.

Children of this age typically know many sight words and are beginning to read more fluently now. It's important to continue to read with your child and have him read to you as well. Seven-year-olds can also write increasingly complex stories. Many children have a mastery of simple addition and subtraction. At home, many transition to solo showers around this age. Insert praise hands emoji!

Capabilities and Limitations

Given that children at this age are a couple of years into school, most are familiar with the expectations of academia and are gaining greater confidence in this setting. They tend to feel great pride in their blossoming abilities and enjoy any opportunity to show them off. Their physical development involves increasing refinement and precision, rather than major ability changes. They are continuing to look longer and leaner, a far cry from the chubby toddlers of just a few years ago. Changes in muscle control, physical development, and brain maturation mean improvements in balance and coordination. Many enjoy activities like riding a bicycle or playing games with friends. Their young bodies still need a variety of healthy food options throughout the day, including snacks between meals. This is an overall healthy time for kids, with less childhood sickness as compared to their younger years, and they're not yet vulnerable to the risks that typically accompany adolescence. Believe it or not, you may actually get to spend more time with your best friend now than with your kid's pediatrician.

Communication

Since your child is now spending much of the day in school and with friends, it's important to take advantage of the in-between times to connect. This may be while you're driving in the car, doing homework together, preparing a meal, or getting ready for bed. To get the conversation flowing, use open-ended questions. For instance, instead of "How was school today?" ask, "What was your favorite part about today?" or "Tell me about a time when you felt excited today." You could also ask about sad or scary times that may have come up while he was at school. Talking about the highs and lows is a great way to get insight into your child's day and help him process his feelings.

DISCIPLINE

Given that discipline is a means to teach children about short-term and long-term goals and values, it's important to have strategies that emphasize problem solving rather than punishment. This way, your child learns to take ownership of choices and behaviors and can look for ways to do things more effectively in the future. Instead of jumping in to fix whatever challenges arise, your job is to express confidence in your child's ability to navigate her own struggles and give her the chance to problem solve on her own. Here's how that worked during one of my nanny jobs: As we were getting ready for a Halloween party, I found Lauren sulking in her bedroom. When I asked what was wrong, she said she'd misplaced the rhinestone face stickers for her princess costume. Instead of quickly scouring the house for them myself, I replied, "Oh, how frustrating! It sounds like you really want those so you can complete your costume. I have a couple of ideas to fix this, but I bet you can come up with some, too. What are some ways we could solve this problem?"

At first Lauren was resistant, but with a bit more prompting, she started to come up with ideas: "I could stay home because my costume sucks, or I could wear my lame costume to the party." Okay, not exactly the positive solutions I was hoping for, but it was a start. She continued, "We could look around the house for the stickers." We decided to divide and conquer; I looked downstairs while she searched upstairs. When we both came up empty-handed, we returned to the problem and looked for more solutions. As we brainstormed, she suggested using markers to draw rhinestones on since the original ones were missing. A fantastic solution! As with Lauren, involving kids in the problem-solving process provides them with tools and coping strategies for facing struggles in the future.

Sibling Rivalry

If you're a parent to two or more children, then you've probably found yourself in the middle of the fighting, yelling, name-calling, or other angry episodes that are part of the sibling rivalry that all brothers and sisters seem to experience. Although it may feel like your children are, at times, each other's worst enemies, they are also each other's best friends. The next time they're bickering over emptying the dishwasher or arguing over the last granola bar, take a deep breath and remind yourself that siblings provide some of the earliest opportunities for our kids to learn empathy, cooperation, and conflict resolution. Isn't that worth witnessing a little nudging and wrestling?

CAUSES

Sibs fight for a variety of reasons. They may be hungry, tired, or bored. They may fight for attention or act out because they feel jealous. This could be due to a change in the family, such as a new baby, or feeling like another sibling gets more recognition from the parents. Kids are in the process of figuring out who they are and how they fit into the family dynamic. When they feel threatened, jealous, angry, misplaced, and so on, they often act out instead of using their verbal communication skills to more appropriately articulate what's going on.

PREVENTION

If you notice an increase in fighting between your children, consider their individual needs for attention and plan one-on-one time with them. Sometimes this may be an afternoon away with each child doing something he or she enjoys, and other times it may be just 10 minutes of uninterrupted play with your older kid while the baby naps.

Avoid using labels with your children, like wild child, athlete, or bookworm. These tags may give your children the mistaken belief that they're locked into a specific way of acting. Help your children utilize "I" messages to more effectively communicate their feelings and needs: for example, "I feel sad when you take my toy away" or "I feel happy when you share your snacks with me."

IN THE MOMENT

When you have to intervene, teach your kids grounding techniques to help them calm down so they can resolve their conflicts in acceptable ways. If necessary—and let's be honest, sometimes it is—remind them that smacking and name-calling don't fall into the category of "acceptable ways." What *can* they do? Count down, take deep breaths, or walk away. Model returning to each other after a fight or disagreement to work things out. Praise kindness, team-work, and cooperation. Show that you value these things, and avoid setting your children up for competition. Give them opportunities to settle their own differences, and only intervene when there's a safety concern.

WHEN THE MOMENT HAS PASSED

Demonstrate patience and understanding with your children. They are still learning conflict resolution skills and effective communication practices. Keep showing them how to do these things, give them special undivided attention, and encourage them to keep up the good work! For more information on creating peaceful, cooperative relationships between your children and within your home, check out the resources listed at the end of this book.

Competition

A couple of months back, my family and I headed to our local BMX track for an evening of competitive bike racing. When the division for seven- and eight-year-olds was

announced, one boy named Jake, a frequent participant in the event, proudly proclaimed, "I'm going to beat all the kids tonight and win the biggest trophy!" He strutted up to the starting gate, prepared to fly past his opponents. When the race ended and he finished second to last, he was devastated and sat sulking at the back of the track for the remainder of the evening.

CAUSES

At this age, children often feel the need to be the fastest, the smartest, the best. They look for ways to prove it, just as Jake expected to do when he declared that he would be the best rider that night. To some degree, we may be socially trained to strive to be the best. We often feel the need to be on the "winning" side and receive validation from this. It's not an inherently good or bad thing, but it can bring undesired outcomes or have a negative impact if taken to an extreme. Our goal for our children should be that they're able to win and lose without getting too hung up on either outcome.

PREVENTION

Whether they're scoring the winning goal in the soccer game or earning the best grade in the class, kids want to shine. Finding ways to encourage this drive in a positive way is important for their self-esteem and social-emotional development. If competition motivates children to improve, promotes teamwork, and encourages practice and preparation, then we can consider this healthy competition.

Get your child involved in sports like soccer, gymnastics, or swimming. Look for group settings where they can work with others and also experience healthy competition. When teams play against each other, the competition may help children see the value of teamwork and cooperation in working toward a goal. This can help children see the merit of working hard, practicing, and striving toward something with a focus on improvement, while also accepting that losing is okay. If your child isn't into sports, a chess club or spelling bee can provide the same practice with competition.

IN THE MOMENT

When Jake lost the race, he dropped his bike on the ground and stormed off the track. Seeing his son's disappointment, Jake's dad sat next to him, and I could hear him validate his son's feelings by saying, "You're mad because you didn't get first place tonight. It's okay to feel upset." A good next step is to help your child develop anger management skills and coping strategies. Ask him, "When you're feeling really upset, what are some things that help you feel better?" It may also be beneficial to point out the progress your child has made: "You were pedaling so fast tonight, and all your practice is really helping in your race start."

WHEN THE MOMENT HAS PASSED
Although it's tempting to avoid situations where your child loses because you fear the dreaded meltdown, try to look for opportunities that give him experience with losing in a supportive environment. For instance, pull out *Chutes and Ladders* and play a round or two with your kid. When your child wins, thank him for a fun game, emphasizing the act of playing rather than the win itself. When you win and your child is upset, empathize with him. Ask him what others might feel when they lose.

Complaining

Back in my nanny days, I loaded the three children I cared for into my car and took them to Chuck E. Cheese for a birthday party. I was young, inexperienced, and completely unaware of the chaos that is Chuck E. Cheese on a Saturday afternoon. We were there for all of five minutes when the complaints started pouring in from all sides: "I'm hungry." "It's cold in here." "This place is for babies." All I could think was, "For the love of all that is good in this world, stop complaining! This is supposed to be fun for you!" Sure, torture for me, but fun for you!

CAUSES

A constant drone of complaints can zap even the patience of a saint. It's draining to hear a barrage of negativity coming from your kid, especially if it seems to be happening on a regular basis. Unfortunately, kids frequently whine and complain because they want something different from what they're getting, and they may have learned that this tactic has worked in the past. Complaining may also be a way for children to manage stress or challenging situations. Though complaining can be part of typical development, there are ways to move your child into more positive thinking.

PREVENTION

I know it's not easy, but try to view complaining as an opportunity to help build problem-solving skills. When your child is complaining of being cold, for instance, say something like, "Hmm. I wonder what you could do to warm up." You can also help your child see the positives: "You feel like Chuck E. Cheese is for younger children like your brother and sister. Look how much they're enjoying the ball pit right now." Provide choices and find ways to allow your child to take ownership: "Would you rather hang out here with me or find a game to play?"

IN THE MOMENT

Take a minute to determine why your child is complaining. Could she be hungry? Tired? Bored? Acknowledge whatever it is that's bothering her. To the child who has informed you 15 bazillion times that she's hungry, reply, "It sounds like you're really hungry. I bet you'll pick a big piece of pizza when it comes out!" Avoid mean-spirited, dismissive comments like "Suck it up, Buttercup" or "Oh, cry me a river." Sometimes children have a difficult time asking for what they want in a positive and productive way. Try responding to them with the positive request version of their statement. For instance, "I'm cold" could be translated into "Could you get me a jacket, please?"

WHEN THE MOMENT HAS PASSED

Point out ways in which your child has successfully navigated a frustrating situation: "You seemed frustrated when we first got to Chuck E. Cheese today because you thought that it was a place for younger kids like your brother and sister. I noticed that after lunch, you played with them in the ball pit, and they loved it!"

If you are concerned that your child's complaints could be a sign of something more serious, such as anxiety or depression, seek medical advice.

Aggression

When I was in high school, I worked as an after-school aide in a kindergarten-through-third-grade program. One student, a second grader named James, was routinely in trouble for his aggressive behaviors. Whether it was shoving, kicking, hitting, throwing items, or even spitting, aggression was part of his daily repertoire. At the time, I had zero knowledge of how to handle this behavior appropriately, so I observed what others did. They often used time-outs, where James was forced to sit at one of the lunch tables instead of playing with the other children. From the table, he often yelled out mean remarks to the children and the adults. At other times, he had to write lines such as "I'll be nice to my friends" over and over. Of course, this usually included a major power struggle, where an adult had to be present to enforce the punishment. Other attempts to tame his angry outbursts included pushups and walks around the playground, standing in a corner for long periods of time, and being sent into the office to wait for his mom to pick him up. Nothing seemed to work.

CAUSES

Looking back, I can see many things that should have been done differently that very likely would have been more effective and certainly more respectful to James. Also, I know that this is not a one-off scenario. There are many kids who regularly struggle with both verbal and physical displays of anger and aggression. And there are many instances in which they are responded to in ways that neither help them learn to do better nor address the long-term goals of discipline.

It's important to remember that all behavior is a form of communication. What is your child trying to say to you through his actions? Is he feeling lonely and rejected? Looking for attention? Anxious because Dad recently moved out? Trying to identify why aggressive behaviors are happening isn't about justifying them, but rather looking for ways to help the child communicate needs more appropriately.

PREVENTION

Make sure that you're not responding to others with anger or yelling, or exhibiting any type of aggressive behavior. Do your best to maintain a calm and supportive atmosphere at home, and model appropriate ways to handle conflict and stress. Acknowledge your child's positive behaviors, and praise him when he regulates his emotions well and responds in appropriate ways. When aggression occurs, take note of when these acts seem to happen. With the million things on a parent's mind, it may be helpful to keep a log of behaviors so you can look for patterns. For instance, do these aggressive episodes occur most often in the after-school program? In a group setting with many children? By making these observations, you may be able to pinpoint what is triggering these reactions.

IN THE MOMENT

So what, exactly, can you do when faced with yet another angry outburst? Of course, it's important to first stay calm. Remember, you set the example for how your child responds in emotional or heated situations. Validate your child's feelings by saying something like, "I can tell you're really angry right now." From there, you can move into finding ways to channel anger more appropriately: "It's okay to be angry. It's not okay to hurt others. When I'm angry, taking a walk helps me calm down. Would you like to take a walk with me?" Ask him if he can think of anything that might help him cool off. Some ideas might include counting down from 10, dancing to silly music, drawing or painting, or even punching a pillow. The goal is to find something that can help alleviate the intensity of his emotions while still allowing him to feel those emotions.

WHEN THE MOMENT HAS PASSED

Kids who experience aggressive episodes in elementary school likely do not have a grasp of effective conflict resolution skills. Help your kid articulate how he's feeling and find constructive ways of solving problems.

Consider potential underlying factors, such as ADHD, anxiety, trauma, autism, sensory processing issues, or learning disorders. If you believe that your child may be impacted by any of these, or if you have concerns, reach out to a medical professional.

Sulking

Janet took her daughter, Lucy, to the store to pick out some decorations for her upcoming birthday party. As they walked through the aisles, Lucy discovered a pair of shoes that she wanted. Janet told her that she couldn't get them and reminded her that, with her birthday coming up, she'd be receiving many gifts. Upon hearing the word "no," Lucy began to pout, sending their shopping trip into Debbie Downer town. Trying to rally despite her daughter's moodiness, Janet headed to another aisle and pointed out balloons and streamers for the party. With her arms folded and bottom lip stuck out as far as it could go, Lucy argued that she didn't even want a party anymore.

CAUSES

It's challenging to deal with the ever-changing emotional states of our kids. One moment they're happy and excited, the next they're pouting in the corner. There are a variety of reasons this occurs. Sometimes kids have trouble expressing their emotions clearly, or they may lack the vocabulary to do so. Kids may sulk because it gets them attention, or in Lucy's case, because she wasn't getting what she wanted. Her disappointment was being communicated through sulking and moodiness.

PREVENTION

Remember that our goal as parents is to raise emotionally balanced adults, not just well-behaved kids. For that reason, maintaining a welcoming, open atmosphere where your child can express feelings is important. Sometimes we all need time and space to channel our inner Eeyore, so try not to feed into your child's moodiness or read too much into it.

IN THE MOMENT

Don't overreact and launch into a lecture. That will just give the sulking more power. Maintain a calm concern and let your child know what you're seeing: "It seems like you're disappointed that I said 'no' to the shoes." Explain that there are other ways of communicating needs and that you're there for her when she's ready: "It looks like you're still upset. Is it because of the shoes earlier today? Would you like to talk about that?" For persistent sulkers who continue long after their feelings have been acknowledged, consider establishing a complaint time and then moving into a no-mope zone: "I understand why you're disappointed and upset. Now is your complaint time, so let me know all about it." After about three to five minutes pass, you can let your child know sulking time is up: "We're playing games as a family right now, so it's a no-mope zone in the family room. Would you like to play here with us, or do something like read or color in your room?"

WHEN THE MOMENT HAS PASSED

When tensions have cooled, consider asking your child about her negative mood. Janet could ask Lucy, "Why do you think you were so upset when I said 'no' to the shoes?" Remind your child that you're there for her no matter what: "I love you, even when you're feeling angry."

A MOMENT OF SANITY

Some days feel like a constant barrage of complaining, arguing, and back talk—with a well-timed eye roll thrown in for good measure. You're not totally sure where that skill was acquired, and you're most certainly not taking credit for it. At times like this, you might feel like hiding out in a closet, praying no one comes searching for you to interrupt your blissful solitude. In fact, if you find yourself needing a moment or two, grab a piece of that dark chocolate you've been hiding and enjoy your closet escape. We won't tell anyone.

Why Me?

AMAYA MADE IT A NIGHTLY PRACTICE to write in her journal, detailing the events of her day. In her latest submission, she wrote, "Dear Diary: Today was a good day. We had a test at school, and I think I did okay. We played kickball during PE and I missed the ball. I'm not very good at sports. My friend, Kelsey, kicked it really far and everyone thought she was so good. We're having a sleepover this weekend and we're going to jump on the trampoline."

Being a typical fourth grader, Amaya is in the process of learning about herself and the things that she enjoys. She loves school, especially hanging out with her friends at recess. She feels confident in academics but is beginning to think of herself as nonathletic. This is a pivotal time in the development of the self, and experiences, both positive and negative, contribute to the way children perceive themselves.

What's New

At this point, your child is well into middle childhood, and it may sometimes seem like she is plowing full steam ahead toward adolescence. The desire for peer acceptance continues to play an increasingly important role, and the friendships established at this age impact the development of self-identity, as well as self-esteem and gender identity. At this age, many children tend to hold fairly rigid and stereotyped views of gender. These are largely based on personal experiences and influenced by the people the children spend the most time with. With their growing independence and desire for peer approval, children often exhibit a greater desire for privacy and space. You may find that your child hangs out in her bedroom behind closed doors more often, and she may also begin to request sleepovers with friends.

Capabilities and Limitations

Physically, kids this age are practicing and refining their skills and need plenty of opportunities for active movement and play. Many children show an increased interest in organized team sports, and other hobbies begin to emerge as children expand upon their own unique interests. Eight-year-olds are typically able to independently take care of their own activities of daily living by bathing, grooming, and dressing themselves.

Children's vocabularies continue to blossom, and they gain greater skills in using their language in creative ways.

Most develop an understanding of irony and begin to use it in their conversations. They have an improving focus and attention span, and an ability to utilize proper grammar most of the time. Their reading skills are becoming more sophisticated. Continue to read to your child, and also have your child read to you.

Communication

Your child is getting older, and your communication style is likely adjusting to reflect this increasing maturity. Set aside time to talk with your child without distractions. By doing this, you are demonstrating the value of your child's opinions and thoughts. Use more Dos than Don'ts, reflecting the behavior that you want to see rather than what you want to avoid. Let your child know when you see helpful and kind actions and behaviors. Since this is considered a pivotal time in your child's burgeoning self-esteem, the way that you talk with your child plays a hugely important role. Emphasize your confidence in your child and her ability to make choices for herself.

DISCIPLINE

Younger kids often struggle to make the connection between their behavior and consequences, especially when they are imposed by an adult. However, at this age, allowing natural and logical consequences to shift your child's behavior may be a helpful approach when used appropriately.

What's the difference between imposed and natural consequences? Natural consequences happen without any adult intervention. For instance, if your child forgot his instrument at home, then he won't be able to participate in band practice later that day. Allowing a natural consequence to take place means that your child experiences the outcomes of his choices or actions without any adult-imposed consequences.

Logical consequences are given by you as a direct result of your child's behavior. To be effective, consequences should be reasonable, related, and respectful. Logical consequences are not punishments. If your child forgets his instrument, a logical consequence might include having to practice for 20 minutes at home later that day, since he wasn't able to at school. Or if he hasn't finished his homework by the time your family usually watches a television show together, a logical consequence might be that he doesn't get to watch the show. These consequences are not a way to mask punishment, but rather a way to connect your child's actions to a related outcome.

COMMON CONUNDRUMS

Chore Wars

You've reminded your child at least 15 times to clean his room, and as you walk in, you find toys and clothes still covering the floor. Your voice and tone escalate, as you insist that this is his final warning. Chore wars rage in nearly all households with children. Chores, the ongoing tasks that need to be done to keep the household running, are often the source of great frustration for parents and children alike.

CAUSES

I can think of at least 10 things I'd rather do than fold the heaping pile of laundry that awaits me tonight. If we're honest, we'll admit that chores really aren't fun. They're often tedious, mundane tasks that need to be done, but they don't usually bring much enjoyment—for parents or children. Kids may avoid these responsibilities because they're boring and they have other things they'd rather be doing. They might also feel overwhelmed by the items on their list or feel like they aren't able to successfully accomplish them.

PREVENTION

When assigning chores, be sure they are age-appropriate and reasonable for your child to accomplish with minimal assistance. For toddlers, that could mean putting toys into bins or tossing dirty clothes into the laundry bin. Preschoolers may be assigned things like putting silverware into the drawer or throwing garbage into the trash can. Common chores for school-age kids include making lunches, doing laundry, folding and putting away clothes, setting the table, helping with dinner preparation, wiping down counters, and washing dishes. Avoid jumping in to "help," even if it means that the task takes longer to complete or is done in ways that you'd do differently. The goal is more about your child contributing to the family's needs than doing something impeccably well.

IN THE MOMENT

Many families use reward systems to get kids on board with doing chores. By completing tasks, kids can earn stars, tokens, or an allowance for their contributions. Or the reward could take the form of a fun outing for the whole family—think going to the movies or having a pool day—at the end of each week or month. If you find that you're repeatedly reminding your child to complete his chores without much action on his part, consider using a reward system that allows for a take-away policy, where the reward is taken away after three reminders or a set time of day at which the tasks have not been done. If after several reminders to tidy his room before dinner, for example, your child has yet to pick up a single item, you may remove a star or dollar. It's important to establish these ground rules beforehand so your child is aware of the consequences, as well as to keep the rules consistent among all family members.

Another idea to move your child into action is to have a set chore time for the entire family, such as 4:00 to 4:30 p.m. every day. You set a timer, and everyone tackles their duties at the same time. Chore time is not just to clean up, but to help children understand their responsibilities within the family.

WHEN THE MOMENT HAS PASSED

Although we can probably agree that tackling a big laundry pile is no fun, as adults we understand that these tasks are not punishments, but rather responsibilities that we have. Keeping that in mind, avoid using chores as punishment for your child. Teach him that, even when it's boring, a job around the house has a purpose. Work together to find ways to complete tasks in a more enjoyable way, like listening to music while doing dishes or creating a game to see how quickly you can pick up toys in the family room.

Asking for an Allowance

Whether it's during a trip to the mall or for those annoying in-app purchases, chances are good that your child has approached you this week looking for some dough for whatever's on her wish list. If the occasional slime sale or lemonade stand isn't keeping up with your child's desire for more pocket money, then an allowance—whether to give it and how much—may be a hot topic in your house.

CAUSES

The "why" here is obvious: Kids want an allowance because they love to spend, spend, spend on candy, books (hopefully!), or whatever the toy or collectible of the moment is (more likely!). There are two general schools of thought when it comes to kids and allowances. One is that children should have an allowance because it helps them learn money management and delayed gratification. The other says children should not have an allowance because it may undermine the value of contributing to the family, providing only extrinsic motivation for completing chores. My thinking is that many household tasks are, and will always be, quite boring. Therefore, I tend to find myself in the camp of using an allowance as a way to motivate kids to complete chores. Regardless of whether an allowance is tied to chores, it provides an opportunity for children to earn money and learn basic financial skills, which is a win-win in my book.

PREVENTION

To prevent doling out an allowance from becoming a head-ache, you, as the parent, get to establish the parameters for your family. You may decide that you want to require a portion be donated or saved to teach your child the value of giving to others or saving for future expenses. You also might want to establish ground rules for what may and may not be purchased with the money. For instance, you might find it important to limit the amount of candy that your child buys each week, or you might prohibit the purchase of toys that resemble weapons. Again, this is specific to your family, but it's important to have this discussion early on and enforce it among all family members.

IN THE MOMENT

Your child is standing before you expectantly waiting to collect. How much do you hand over? Although the amount may depend on each family's financial situation and loca-tion, one general rule is fifty cents or one dollar per year of age per week. That means an eight-year-old would get four or eight dollars per week. With this approach, there's an automatic bump up at each birthday, eliminating any con-cern children may have about a raise or keeping things fair between siblings. It also gives you a ready answer when-ever your child peppers you with requests for more money. If there's a situation where your child asks for money in advance (perhaps you're on vacay and that's his only chance to snag that souvenir), consider keeping the item until the debt has been paid, having him sign an IOU, or holding a possession of similar value until the debt is paid.

WHEN THE MOMENT HAS PASSED

Whether it's allowance day or not, remember, it's your call whether your child gets an allowance, when it's given, and how it may be used. If you decide to move forward with an allowance, talk with your child about the reasons for it and the expectations surrounding it.

Impatience

Recently, we had a family pool day planned that we were all very excited about, especially my daughter. She went to bed clutching her bathing suit, promptly put it on when she awoke at 6 a.m., and asked me at least a hundred times before breakfast if it was time to go yet. Still several hours away from leaving and exasperated from the incessant "Is it time now?!," I curtly said, "Stop asking! I'll tell you when it's time." When it comes to impatience—theirs and occasionally my own—I have a lot of daily experience. And that's why I'm beginning to think that kids and patience are mutually exclusive.

CAUSES

The ability to delay gratification is a critical component of patience, and this is something that adults and children alike struggle with. In many ways, we are a very instant-gratification-seeking society. Just the other day, my friend told me about a new skincare product that promises to make my tired eyes look younger and fresher. Within two minutes, it was in my Amazon cart, checked out, and on its way to my front door. We want things, and we want them now. Consider the last time you had to wait in a long line at the grocery store or found yourself cursing your computer because of incredibly slow-loading web pages. Heaven forbid there's no Wi-Fi and we can't get an answer from Google in two milliseconds.

My point is, we are often impatient, and our children are, too. The difference is that they have a bit of an excuse, given their age and developmental stage. Their young brains are still developing and greatly benefit from seeing positive examples of patience.

PREVENTION

Look for frequent, small opportunities when you can delay gratification and build patience. Perhaps your child wants a new toy that she's been eyeing for several weeks. You could purchase it and give it to her now, but you could also buy it and wait until her birthday in two weeks. Another great way to bulk up those patience muscles is to practice turn taking in your home. Having to wait to play with a toy or use an item delays gratification and often creates some discomfort for your child. This is okay! It helps children get used to the feeling of waiting for something they want.

IN THE MOMENT

When my daughter repeatedly asked if we were heading to the pool yet, it would have been better if I had responded with "You must be excited! You've asked me many times if it's time to go. I'll come and find you when we're ready to leave after lunch."

As another example, say that your child is losing it because it's going to take *forever* for dinner to be ready. Instead of handing her a snack to appease her, say something along the lines of "Oh, you're so hungry! I wonder what you'll eat first at dinner, the carrots or the rice." Acknowledge your child's desire and need—she probably *is* hungry and wants food now—but realize that with only 15 more minutes until dinner is ready, this a prime time to hone those patience-building skills.

WHEN THE MOMENT HAS PASSED
Encourage turn taking through games, particularly ones that increase distress tolerance or the ability to manage a stressful situation you can't change. Good picks include Jenga (will the pieces all crash down?!), Kerplunk, or even checkers or chess. These games give kids opportunities to put patience into practice. Know that it takes time, modeling, and plenty of experience to become better at waiting. You can probably think of some adults who are still learning to do this!

Trouble with Impulse Control

One Sunday morning as the offering plate was passed through the congregation at church, eight-year-old Jeremiah saw the money in the basket, and without processing his actions, reached in and grabbed a handful of bills. He quietly pocketed the money and glanced around to see if anyone had noticed. Later that day, when his mom discovered the extra cash, she questioned him about where it came from. She was appalled to learn that he had stolen it from the church.

CAUSES

Impulsivity, or acting without thinking and purposeful intention, is common among all ages. This may be attributed to the fact that certain regions of the brain are still developing up until the mid-twenties. The prefrontal cortex, the area behind the forehead, is responsible for planning, prioritizing, empathy, and impulse control, among other important tasks. Over time, these improving executive function skills make it easier for your child to delay gratification and display impulse control.

Kids struggle with impulse control throughout their childhood, and this can range from grabbing a toy away from another child as a preschooler, stealing without considering the consequences in elementary school, or sharing inappropriate photos on social media as a preteen or adolescent. Impulsivity may involve taking excessive or unnecessary risks, speaking before thinking, interrupting others while in conversation, having trouble waiting turns, or even acting aggressively. Your child may push her way into the front of the line, hit or throw items when frustrated, or constantly interrupt your conversation. Things like stress, frustration, fatigue, and hunger may cause a child to act more impulsively. Temperament and energy levels may also play a role.

PREVENTION

Help your child tap into executive function skills by problem solving together and coming up with solutions to troublesome situations. For example, if your child frequently interrupts conversation, you might encourage her to place her hand on your arm to gain your attention in a less intrusive way. Brainstorm similar solutions for however your child's impulsivity tends to express itself.

IN THE MOMENT

After you get past the thought "What on earth was my kid thinking?," try to consider the factors that contributed to his action. Jeremiah's mom was understandably upset, but she might consider that he's been saving up his allowance for a new skateboard, and the temptation—in the form of a basket of bills—was right in front of him. With this in mind, she can tell him, "It's not okay to take things that don't belong to you, and I think you know that. My guess is that you saw the money and took some without really thinking about what that means. I know you've been saving for that new skateboard for a while, so it might have been especially tempting."

WHEN THE MOMENT HAS PASSED

In the case of Jeremiah, his mom could explain why his action was wrong and take him to return the money: "It's not okay to take things from others, including money from the offering. This afternoon we're going to head to church and give this back to the pastor, together."

Talk with your child about the concerning behavior, focusing on finding a solution to a situation like this in the future. You may find the book *What Were You Thinking? Learning to Control Your Impulses,* by Bryan Smith, helpful. This story follows a third grader who struggles with controlling his impulses at school, sometimes hurting others' feelings in the process.

Note that ADHD, other disorders, and mental health issues may lead children to act more impulsively. It's important to seek professional advice if you're concerned about your child's impulsive behaviors.

Screaming for Screen Time

Because technology and screen media have exploded only recently, we don't have the benefit of knowledge and wisdom passed down from previous generations. Instead, we're finding ourselves in a new world of determining what healthy technology use looks like in our own families. There are undoubtedly benefits of being able to connect with others near and far, but there are certainly drawbacks as well.

Research reveals a number of negative impacts of screen time, especially long periods of exposure, including sleep disturbances, behavioral problems, violence and aggression, educational challenges, obesity, and more. Screen time may desensitize the brain's reward system and induce stress reactions by overloading the sensory system. It has been shown to impair attention and increase impulsivity and aggression. On top of that, screen media exposes our kids to commercials and marketing that their young brains are ill-equipped to fully process.

CAUSES

From playing a video game or watching a television program to mindlessly scrolling through social media and online shopping, screens captivate us and addict us. They offer us a reward, a pleasurable experience in which we easily find ourselves lost.

PREVENTION

Establish places in your home where screens are allowed and where they aren't allowed. Keep screens in shared spaces, and avoid having TVs, computers, and other devices in bedrooms—yours included. It may feel like you're punishing yourself, but not only are you setting a good example, you're boosting your own well-being. This is another tough one, but avoid giving your child personal devices. I know it's hard to say no when "everyone" else has them. If your child does have personal devices, at least consider having a docking station where all electronics go for charging and storage.

Set up guidelines for when your child can use a screen. For instance, consider eliminating screens during meals or while in the car. These are great times to connect with your child, and that won't happen with devices in hand.

IN THE MOMENT

If you've already tried the prevention measures and you need help prying your kids away from the screen time they are allowed to have, try this approach. Get into your child's world by asking a question about what he's doing: "Can you show me how this game works?" "What's going on with this girl in the show?" Create a dialogue and then help ease your child back into the real world. Once you've begun a conversation, let your child know that there are five minutes left until it's time to disconnect. Remember, screens produce a state of pleasure, and the goal of this practice is to connect with your child and help transition his brain back to the real world.

WHEN THE MOMENT HAS PASSED

Encourage activities that promote movement and creativity. Go outside and play together. Set aside unplugged time, value it, and model it for your child. Consider placing time restrictions on screen usage, and let your child know that too much screen time is unhealthy.

A MOMENT OF SANITY

Our kids, more than anyone else in the world, have the ability to send us right over the edge. As you move through this season of parenting, it may be helpful to take a little time each day (hide in the laundry room if you must!) to write down some of the highs and lows. Even just a few minutes alone with your thoughts, something that's admittedly hard to come by with little ones around, can help you become more calm, cool, and collected. And on particularly frustrating days, this reflective time can give you a chance to remember the positives, like that one time your child actually did listen. Hallelujah!

9 YEAR OLDS

Is That Normal?!

AS AMY AND HER NINE-YEAR-OLD SON, Max, were finishing up their evening homework routine, Max commented that no one else in his class liked math. He went on to say that it was his favorite subject, but he couldn't let anyone in his class know this, otherwise they might think he was a nerd. Like many kids at this age, Max understood his own interests, talents, and preferences, but he was also keenly aware of the opinions of others.

What's New

Although the ability to empathize with and relate to others improves as kids reach the end of their single-digit years, they continue to have a focus on themselves, especially concerning others' perceptions of them. Impending puberty only serves to exacerbate these thoughts and leads many to alter their appearance in order to fit into social circles.

Around this age, children seek more relationships outside of the family, which often includes having a best friend, especially for girls. Both boys and girls tend to prefer same-sex playmates. Sleepovers often become a common occurrence around this age, and with your child's blossoming social life, you may begin to feel like you're taking a backseat in your kid's world. Although kids are starting to focus more on outside relationships, especially as they head toward the teen years, know that your child still greatly depends on you for comfort and support as he navigates his increasing independence.

Capabilities and Limitations

With puberty on the horizon, many nine-year-olds begin to experience growth spurts. This tends to happen earlier for girls than for boys. You can expect kids this age to be more independent in caring for themselves, which includes things such as bathing, dressing, preparing meals, and feeding themselves. Kids may show greater interest in team and individual sports as their physical strength, coordination, and balance improve. They enjoy practicing and honing their skills.

At nine, children are using adult-like grammar and are generally understood well by strangers. You may notice that your child is using more figurative expressions, and he may even use slang picked up from peers—which means you'll now be the "old" person who has no idea what some of these terms mean. How did that happen so fast? Kids this age also tend to use long and complex sentences and have a firm grasp on comparative language; many school assignments require extensive writing that reflect this. Academics may become more of a challenge as learning shifts from the play-centered approach that ruled during the younger years.

Communication

Your child is navigating the complex world of friendships (and the occasional enemy), and this often means that there are hurt feelings and disappointments. Take care to show empathy and recognize that your child's experiences are difficult. By validating her feelings, you're continuing to build your relationship and reinforce open communication. Don't take it as a bad sign if it sometimes feels like you're pulling teeth trying to have a conversation with your kid. This is typical at this stage of development, and it means that she's maturing and moving toward greater autonomy. If she seems especially tight-lipped, try opening up about your own day, sharing things that happened to you, like an important meeting at work or a funny incident at the grocery store. This can serve as a conversation starter, as it takes the pressure off your child to spill the details of her day. After you break the ice and get the conversation flowing, your child might interrupt to describe events that happened during her day.

DISCIPLINE

As your child moves into the preteen years, she is becoming more independent, and the discipline strategies that you used when she was younger may not be as effective. Establishing clear boundaries and expectations is crucial. Explain these expectations ahead of time, and be clear on the reasons behind the rules. A great way to get your child involved is to have family meetings where your preteen can take part in the decision-making process. Jane Nelsen, a marriage and family counselor and author of numerous books on positive discipline strategies, argues that this is one of the most important things you can do, because it keeps the lines of communication open and gives all family members a chance to talk about concerns in a nonthreatening environment. In this setting, mistakes and struggles are viewed as an opportunity for learning and growth. A family meeting works especially well as children get older, because it allows them to have a say in the rules and expectations. When issues come up, they go on the agenda to be discussed at the meeting. This way, all family members can bring their concerns to the table and work together to come up with solutions. Make the meeting purposeful and fun. Schedule the time for once a week, maybe after dinner. You could have dessert or an after-dinner snack while you meet. Give each person an opportunity to bring up concerns, as

well as possible solutions to these issues. For more information on family meetings and how to implement them within
your own family, check out the resources listed at the end of
this book (page 153).

(page 153)

COMMON CONUNDRUMS

Laziness

It's a daily struggle to get Miles to clean his room, write a
thank you note to his grandparents, or find his own hoodie
in the laundry pile. Regardless of the task, he seems to lack
motivation to do anything productive, preferring to spend
idle time engrossed in video games or holed up in his room.
Exhausted from the constant battle to get Miles to take care
of his responsibilities, his parents often feel like they're at
their wits' end. They've tried reminders and chore charts,
nagged and yelled, taken away privileges, and nothing
seems to work. Sound familiar? Maybe some new insights
can help.

CAUSES

Though it may appear that Miles is lazy and neglectful of
his responsibilities, his actions (or lack thereof) likely communicate something else. Children who lack confidence in
their abilities or are discouraged, frustrated, or disinterested
may shirk tasks and responsibilities. Your child may be
overwhelmed by a homework task, and therefore pretend to
not care about school. When a task feels too challenging, it's
easier to check out with other activities, such as watching

TV or playing video games, than tackle what needs to be done. Even as adults we do this. Who hasn't zoned out by scrolling through Instagram or bingeing on Netflix to avoid jumping into a task that seems overwhelming? Even as I've been writing this book, I've found myself getting lost in an Internet black hole, especially when I should be working on the more challenging sections.

PREVENTION

Model the motivation that you'd like to see in your child. Do you want him to clean his room? Keep other areas of the house tidy. Do you want him to do his homework without a fight? Demonstrate that this is a priority by establishing a set time and place where this will be done each day. Set him up for success by giving him the tools, resources, and modeling that he needs. Find things that are motivating, like listening to music while cleaning the cat's litter box or giving him his allowance after the completion of specified tasks.

IN THE MOMENT

Get to the underlying reasons for your child's lack of motivation, and work together to come up with solutions. Using Miles as an example, his parents are frustrated that he's not cleaning his room, so they can write this issue on the family meeting agenda. When everyone is together, Dad might say, "In our house, it's important to keep rooms tidy. It seems like you find this rule unfair, and you're having a hard time keeping your room clean. Let's come up with some solutions to this issue. Miles, what are some ideas that you have?"

Miles might say that one solution is just to shut his bedroom door. You don't need to approve or shut down any solutions in this phase; it's just a period of brainstorming. Everyone gets an opportunity to chime in. Other ideas might include having bins for items to be thrown into, making the space a bit tidier. You could set a timer for 20 minutes and clean together. He could be expected to clean once on the weekend but leave his bedroom as-is during the weekdays. Find solutions you're all comfortable with.

WHEN THE MOMENT HAS PASSED
Shift your mindset away from thinking of your child as lazy, because in reality, he is most likely anxious, overwhelmed, or distracted. For kids to work on something that feels especially challenging or boring, they need to have a healthy level of self-competence, meaning that they believe that they can succeed with continued effort. Motivation begins with interest. If you're interested in something, you are much more likely to invest time and energy in it.

Homework Battles

For DeShon, the time between the end of school and bedtime is usually overflowing with things that need to be accomplished. Dinner, homework, piano lesson, karate, shower time—it's no wonder his family is feeling a bit frazzled. His dad, frustrated by DeShon's dawdling when it comes to completing his assignments, angrily reminds his son that he needs to finish his homework before their family meal. With jam-packed days leaving little room for downtime, a perfect storm for homework resistance is born.

CAUSES

There are a number of reasons why you may be facing a nightly homework battle in your home. Like DeShon, many children are mentally taxed and exhausted from a long day at school, wanting some downtime once they get home. As adults, we're no different; we eagerly await the clock ticking five so we can head out and unwind from a long day. For kids, another possible issue is that they're bored with the work, or, conversely, they may find it too challenging.

PREVENTION

Build homework into your family's routine, and carve out some time that is calm with minimal distractions. If there are other family members present who don't have homework, they should be engaging in other quiet activities. It can be torture for a child to sit still for 40 minutes' worth of math problems when a sibling is enjoying loud video games in the next room. A set quiet time each day dedicated to completing homework together provides routine and structure that your child will come to know and predict. By keeping the emphasis on learning together and providing an atmosphere that is conducive to this, you set up your child for success.

Have kids do homework in a common area of the home, like the dining room, kitchen, or family room, and focus on connecting through homework. View it as a valuable part of your time together. If you come into the setting feeling anxious and in a rush to get it done, your mood transfers onto your child. While considering your schedule and your family's needs, you may find it helpful to offer a snack before or during the homework session. Try adding some light stretching routines beforehand to get bodies and minds focused for work and concentration.

IN THE MOMENT
Okay, deep breath. Yes, this is super frustrating for parents. Note that silently (no need to totally stuff that feeling down), and acknowledge your child's feelings. Explain the reasons behind the assignments and remind your child of the expectations regarding homework. As you and your child work together, make it a collaborative effort and allow your child to "teach" you. When she's feeling frustrated or overwhelmed by complex tasks, remind her of the power of "not yet," meaning that it takes time and practice to fully grasp the concept. When your child says she can't do something, rephrase it as she can't do it *yet*. Keep your child's temperament in mind, and use it to guide your approach. What works for one child may not work for another. For a kid who tends to procrastinate, consider holding off on doing fun activities until the homework is done. For a child who becomes obsessed with and stuck in striving for perfection, emphasize the process of completing assignments, rather than the overall product. Learning comes through the doing, not the final outcome.

WHEN THE MOMENT HAS PASSED
Remember that it's not entirely on you to get your child to succeed in school. Don't get stuck in a power struggle or battle of wills, as this isn't conducive to learning or

completing homework tasks. Although our job is to teach and coach our children in their learning and in their homework, we can also let them experience the natural, as well as logical, consequences of not doing homework.

Stubbornness

Sofia is the classic strong-willed child. She knows what she wants, and she's not going to let a little thing like her parents' instructions stand in her way. When her mom, Carolina, told her to wear her new dress to her grandmother's 80th birthday party, she refused to change out of the jeans and sweatshirt she was already wearing. The family ended up being late to the gathering as Carolina alternately argued, negotiated, and finally yelled at Sofia to change her clothes. Her parents may grudgingly admire her conviction, but constantly fighting with her is leaving them emotionally drained and wondering "Who does this kid think she is, anyway?"

CAUSES

Children have a need for power and a sense of control over their own lives, and this often results in arguing, yelling, and defiance. Questioning authority is typical and expected of kids, especially around this age and as they move into their teenage years. Some children may display more argumentativeness and rebellion than others.

PREVENTION

When a child's argumentativeness is met with arguing, yelling, or attempts at control, a power struggle is created and that's not good news for you or your child. The more you argue, the more the interaction escalates, making it difficult for either of you to accomplish anything productive. Instead, acknowledge the motive for your child's behavior. Consider if you could be wrong (hey, it happens to the best of us), and apologize when you're wrong about something or if you reacted inappropriately. Watch your own tone, and consider how you speak to your child. Be a good listener. Children (and people in general) are much less defensive and combative when they feel heard and understood. Work together to solve problems, and always view yourself and your child as being on the same team.

IN THE MOMENT

When you hear the feisty tone emerging, remind your child of your expectations: "It's okay for us to disagree, but it needs to be done respectfully." This is something that we want for our children throughout their entire lives, to be able to respectfully disagree with others and have an open dialogue with them. Avoid making empty threats such as, "If you don't clean up your room right now, I'm going to throw away all your toys." If those words are coming out of your mouth, you should be prepared to enter the room with trash bags to start tossing items. Pick your battles. When it's one that you're willing to fight for, be clear about your expectations, as well as the consequences.

Strong-willed children have an intense desire for control in their lives; consequently, they love to have choices: "Would you like to go to bed now or in five minutes? Okay, five minutes it is. It's sometimes hard to go to bed, especially when you're having fun playing. What will help you get to bed more easily when the five minutes are up?" Problem solve together, especially when it's outside of a heated moment. Consider bringing it to a family meeting to discuss and come up with solutions.

Yelling

As Shelly was making dinner in the kitchen, her kids were playing in the family room nearby. What started out as relatively quiet chatter turned into an all-out yelling match between her children. Having reminded them to quiet down several times, she found her own volume increasing to the point where she wondered if her neighbors heard the turmoil in her home.

CAUSES

Yelling is not inherently bad. There are times and places when it's very appropriate to raise your volume and intensity, like at a sporting event or in the face of danger. However, there are other times when it's not the best response. Here's the thing, though: Yelling is effective because it commands attention. And if we're being honest, when we yell at our kids, it's likely because they didn't hear us—or at least that's what they claim—the first five times we spoke and we want their attention. Our children are not

much different. If they don't get the response they want, they may raise their voice out of frustration and anger.

PREVENTION

As with most behaviors, modeling is our best bet in terms of curbing the screaming. Show your child what it looks like to feel angry without exploding and to feel frustrated without emotional outbursts. Help your child find more appropriate—and lower volume—ways of asking for attention.

IN THE MOMENT

Listen to what your child is trying to communicate through the screaming. Although it may be tempting to yell in response to your child's escalations, find a way to calm yourself before speaking. Raising your voice in response to your child's yelling doesn't demonstrate the behavior that you want to see. Even when it feels like a struggle, when you slip up and shout more than you'd like, continue to practice pausing before reacting. When shouting is the default setting that's been in place for many decades, it takes time to retrain the brain.

WHEN THE MOMENT HAS PASSED
Wait until the situation has calmed down before you try to address it. An angry, yelling child is not coming from a rational place. Once things have settled down, maybe later in the evening, sit down next to your child to chat with him. Shelly could say, "Earlier today when I was making dinner, you were yelling a lot and seemed really angry. What was going on then? Can you think of some ways you could handle it differently in the future?" Brainstorm with your child about solutions for the future, giving him the tools he needs to successfully navigate big emotions next time. If you do yell, apologize to your child after the tension has subsided.

Lying

Usually one to spend the night before a test studying, Marta felt unprepared for the big history exam that day because she'd been busy with a family birthday party. When it came time to take the test after lunch, Marta placed her sheet with notes on it on the floor next to her desk so that she could glance at it if she didn't know the answer to a question. When Marta's teacher suspected her of cheating during the test, she confronted Marta, who adamantly insisted that she wasn't cheating, but rather that she was just looking for her eraser, which she'd dropped on the floor.

Kids tell lies throughout childhood, but in contrast to the days of early childhood, the lies now have likely gotten smoother and more refined, leaving you surprised by how easily falsehoods seem to roll off your child's tongue. To make matters more challenging, it may seem like there's a new secretiveness surrounding your preteen's life, given that she's not as willing to share the latest events at school. This is developmentally appropriate and expected, and is considered to be a sign of growing maturity. If you want to revisit how to handle lying with younger kids, refer to page 21.

CAUSES

Kids and adults lie for the same reasons. We lie because we've made mistakes, we're afraid of punishment, we want to fit in, or we want to get out of something we don't want to do. Marta felt unprepared for a test, but she wanted to get a good grade. She decided to cheat on the test and then lie about it, even though she knew it would disappoint her teacher and parents and that cheating would likely result in negative consequences, like a failing grade on the test.

PREVENTION

Model honesty, even if this means paying for a more expensive admission to a theme park when your child could probably pass for a younger age. You play an important role in showcasing honesty. Set your children up for honesty, and be a source of help and support when there are lies: "It's not okay to lie about cheating (or stealing, skipping home-work, pushing your brother, etc.). I'm upset about this, but I love you."

IN THE MOMENT

In Marta's case, her teacher wants her to be honest about the cheating. By calmly seeking to understand why the child has lied, the teacher can set the stage for a teachable moment. Marta's teacher could have responded, "I'm curious if you weren't honest about the test because you were feel-ing embarrassed and afraid of what the consequences might be. I expect you to be honest with me."

WHEN THE MOMENT HAS PASSED

Remind your child that you love her no matter what and that you want to work together to find solutions. Marta's teacher could ask, "What are some things that you could do the next time you're feeling nervous about a test?" Help your child realize that there are always better solutions than lying.

A MOMENT OF SANITY

As your child approaches the preteen years, you'll likely find that she is eager to assert her independence. So you know what? This is the perfect time to remind yourself what it feels like to do what you want. After all, you're the adult, and you actually can go out with your friends when you want. So book a table at the hot new restaurant in town, make a date to see the latest blockbuster, or even enjoy a solo outing. Remember what it's like to take off the parent hat and enjoy some hard-earned R&R.

10 YEAR OLDS

Don't Judge Me

FIFTH GRADE WAS TOUGH FOR SIENNA. As puberty approached, her body began changing. Her mom insisted that she start using deodorant and got her a bra, which she was convinced everyone could tell she was wearing. She had her first crush and was devastated when a boy in her class revealed her romantic feelings to the entire school. Most days were filled with uncertainty, embarrassment, and fear that others were judging her.

You remember being 10, don't you? That awkward time when you desperately want to fit in with your friends, while you're not even sure you fit in your own body. Society considers 10-year-olds to be in the tween stage—that exciting, nerve-racking land between childhood and adolescence. This is the time of unrequited crushes, acne-prone skin, and a body that seems to be morphing before your eyes.

What's New

Many kids, especially girls, begin to enter puberty around this time. However, like nearly all stages of development, there is a range of what is considered typical. The onset of puberty may bring a wide array of emotions, such as excitement, embarrassment, and nervousness. Girls tend to grow faster and are often taller than boys at this age (just look back at your fifth-grade class photo and you'll see what I'm talking about). The surge in hormones at this time is usually accompanied by increased sweating, oily and acne-prone skin, and hair growth under the arms and around the genital area. Girls may begin to experience breast growth, whereas boys may experience growth of the penis and testicles. Kids benefit from continued conversations about sexuality and sexual development so they know what to expect and how to manage the changes.

Rapid growth means kids often have an increased appetite and the need for more sleep. They may complain of muscle cramps or growing pains. It's not uncommon for body image issues or concerns to begin around this age, although the foundation for self-esteem has been laid long before this point.

Most kids continue to have a best friend, typically of the same sex. Meanwhile, crushes and young romantic interests are often budding, but most kids are embarrassed at the thought of revealing them. Friends may form cliques, although this is more common among girls. As the desire to fit in skyrockets, peer pressure increases. At this age, kids tend to show greater interest in and awareness of current events, as well as pop culture. They likely have favorite singers, bands, sports teams, and movies.

Capabilities and Limitations

Ten-year-olds have improved speed, balance, and coordination, making team games and sports even more competitive and exciting. The amount of homework usually increases, with more advanced topics and assignment expectations as kids prepare to head into middle school. They can read and understand paragraphs of complex sentences and are reading chapter books. Capable of more logical and abstract thinking, they're learning how to research and analyze information.

Kids are improving in their conflict resolution skills. They still experience mood swings, which may make them seem mature one moment and irrational the next. They may start questioning authority, idolize older children and adolescents, and experience more intense peer pressure, all of which are part of typical development.

Communication

Communicating with a preteen often involves silence, shrugs, and sighs. Your child may even start to be embarrassed by your presence. Although she likely wants more privacy, and it's appropriate to provide that to some extent, don't let this discourage you from regularly reaching out to her. If you find that your child seems more distant and preoccupied, you're not alone. Try talking to her while you do activities together, like playing a game or going on a bike ride. Shared activities can help promote closeness, even if minimal words are exchanged. Listen to your child's opinion and perspective, demonstrate respect, and provide kind but firm reminders of expectations. You're continuing to lay the foundation for open communication, which is crucial as you enter into the often rebellious and isolating years of adolescence. Your role as a parent is shifting and changing, but know that your kid still needs your love, support, and guidance.

DISCIPLINE

Sometimes, when one of my children is driving me absolutely nuts, I think back to the movie *Mean Girls* and channel my inner Mrs. George. I remind myself that I'm not like a regular mom. I'm a cool mom. Only in this case, I'm not talking about wearing a pink velour track suit and inappropriately trying to be BFFs with my teenager. I'm reminding myself that I have the choice to *keep my cool*—to be calm and responsive—instead of being intense and reactive. Don't get me wrong, there are many times when I'm so angry, I feel like I'm one eye roll away from total combustion. In these moments, it's especially important to remind myself that I have a choice in how I respond. I'm not responsible for my kid's emotional outbursts and angst, but I am responsible for my own actions.

Training yourself to experience your feelings without acting on them in anger takes lots of time and practice. I'll be the first to admit that I sometimes lose my temper and yell at my kids in heated moments. It's happened before, and I'm sure it will happen again. Be gracious with yourself and with your kids. Get back up and try again. And don't underestimate the power of venting to friends who get it. The preteen hijinks that are supremely frustrating in the moment can often seem innocuous and, dare I say it, even humorous over a round of margaritas at parents' night out.

Body Image

One time when Christy was younger, she was at the pool with her dad and her friend Kenna. Christy was keenly aware of how her body contrasted with Kenna's thinner frame. At one point, Christy's dad hoisted Kenna high up into the air and then tossed her into the water. Christy eagerly shouted, "Me next!" When her dad replied, "Sorry sweetheart, you're too big," she was devastated. These words stuck with her and impacted her ever since. Now, at 10, Christy feels uncomfortable in her body and is ashamed of the way she looks.

CAUSES

Most women today are unhappy with their bodies or features of their appearance. Like Christy, many of us have early memories of when we first became aware of and dissatisfied with our own bodies. We judge our appearance harshly and then pray that our kids won't experience this same self-hatred.

Research indicates that children as young as three years old dislike their bodies. Three years old! Let that sink in for a moment. Another scary fact: Some girls as young as four feel the need to lose weight and have even learned ways to do this, such as skipping meals. This is heartbreaking. We tend to think about body image struggles as a prepubescent and adolescent issue, but the way children view themselves is heavily set before they even enter kindergarten. That image often lasts for many decades, if not a lifetime. Of course, this is a complex issue with many contributing factors. One might argue that media, with its unrealistic portrayals of people, plays a pivotal role. Advertising and marketing capitalize on the things we don't like about ourselves, because it's hugely profitable for companies. We are constantly bombarded by images and opinions about how we should look. The best way to combat this barrage is by modeling a positive sense of self at home.

PREVENTION

If we want our children to love, appreciate, and value their bodies, then we must do the same for our own. The goal is to instill in our children the belief that self-worth is not dependent on physical characteristics. To do this, we must believe it and act it daily. How? Watch your words. Avoid commenting negatively on your own body. Steer clear of referring to yourself as fat or needing to diet. Instead of saying that you need to lose 10 pounds to be ready for swimsuit season, just put on the swimsuit and have fun at the pool. If you eat ice cream after dinner with the family, don't comment on how you'll need to work that off tomorrow. Just enjoy the ice cream and move on. Focus on health and behavior instead of fixating on appearance. Weight is only one measure of health, so don't neglect the other areas.

IN THE MOMENT

If you're like me and have struggled with liking your physical appearance, know that it's never too late to switch to a new path, one in which you learn to love your body. Eat healthy. You'll feel better, and your kids will model this behavior. Find a physical activity that's fun for you. Always wanted to take dance lessons? Make a pact with your partner to trade off kid time so you can fit in lessons and he can get out on his mountain bike for a few hours a week. Keep in mind that your comments and actions are profoundly powerful, not only to your observing child, but also to the way that you view yourself. Help your child discover ways to appreciate her body for what it can do, rather than what it looks like.

WHEN THE MOMENT HAS PASSED

If your child seems concerned about a certain physical feature, like how her stomach looks in a bathing suit, for instance, help her connect to other characteristics that she likes, such as her strong legs that propel her down the soccer field. Take a moment to review toys, books, movies, and other media to see what types of bodies and physical characteristics are being portrayed. When you see an ad that portrays people in unrealistic ways, ask your child about it. We can't prevent our children from seeing all media, but we can talk with them about what they're viewing. Maintaining an open dialogue about body change is important, as is keeping screen time to a minimum.

If you seriously struggle with self-esteem and body image issues, consider seeking help from a mental health professional.

Cyber Safety

Noah and a friend spent the night at another friend's house. When Noah arrived home, his mom, Candace, noticed that Noah seemed a bit more quiet than usual. Candace asked about the sleepover, but her son remained tight-lipped. After dinner, Noah revealed that he and the other boys had looked at porn when the adults had gone to bed. Candace began to panic, unsure of how to respond to this news.

CAUSES
Most tweens today walk around with smartphones, laptops, and tablets in their backpacks. Although they're a tech-savvy generation, they often lack sound judgment when it comes to cyber safety, due to their age and cognitive abilities. The easy availability of technology opens the door for risks such as cyberbullying, sexting, and viewing pornography and other content that's inappropriate for young ones. The unfortunate reality is that tweens who surf the web unsupervised are likely to come across content that's not intended for them.

PREVENTION
To minimize the likelihood of your child stumbling upon inappropriate content, keep devices in a shared area of your home, like the family room. Set up parental controls that restrict access to certain websites, and utilize search

engines that are kid friendly, like Kiddle or KidzSearch. When helping your child set up online accounts or profiles, create a username that doesn't include your child's real name. Don't include any photos that identify your home or your child's school. (Watch out for information giveaways, like your child wearing a T-shirt with the name of his school or town on it.) Make sure your child knows never to share personal information online. Talk with him about interacting with people online, stressing that he should never talk to strangers. Teach him that people can disguise themselves online and pretend to be someone they're not.

Talk to your child about what to do if there are ever messages or things that make him feel uncomfortable. Share an e-mail account with your child. If your child wants to use social media and you give the green light, consider creating an account that is shared by the two of you. This gives him the opportunity to practice digital literacy skills in a low-risk, safe environment, given that you are closely monitoring content.

IN THE MOMENT

Encourage your child to come to you with anything that makes her feel uncomfortable or threatened. Don't freak out about things that she shares. Or, more realistically, stay calm on the outside while secretly freaking out on the inside. Whatever comes up can be a learning opportunity to give your child additional skills in navigating the digital world. Noah's mom might say, "The photos and videos that you saw at the sleepover are not appropriate for kids. I'm glad that you're sharing this with me, and I'd like to talk about it more tonight." Feel free to have a glass of wine before you pick up that conversation!

WHEN THE MOMENT HAS PASSED
If your child has discovered inappropriate content online or has engaged in risky Internet activities, it's important to keep a composed demeanor and analyze the situation. Consider how and why your child got access to this material. Avoid shaming your child for what he saw. Rather, use this as an opportunity to discuss online safety, and perhaps sexuality, more thoroughly. You can open the conversation with "It might have been overwhelming to see those images. Do you have any questions about what you saw? Is there anything you'd like to talk about?"

Back Talk

Being on the receiving end of a barrage of back talk is exhausting to the core. Whether it's your son shouting "You're not the boss of me!" as he storms into his room or your daughter muttering "You just don't understand" under her breath, complete with a dramatic eye roll, back talk is one of the most maddening aspects of parenting. All children engage in it at some point in their formative years, usually more than once.

CAUSES
Much like whining and complaining, which we talked about on pages 68 and 86, respectively, back talk should be viewed as a form of communication, albeit a disrespectful

and obnoxious one. Back talk is not very effective, in that it often comes across as hostile and rude, but its use does give us an opportunity to teach our kids better ways of letting their needs be known. Sometimes back talk is an indicator of a child who is trying to exert control over his own life. It's not uncommon for children to often feel helpless and powerless, like they don't have much say in their lives. When that happens, be prepared for some saltiness. Part of their job as children is to push boundaries and lean in to the limits that parents establish. At the same time, your role as a parent is to establish limits and ground rules for your child, as well as your entire family.

PREVENTION

Establish appropriate and expected behavior by speaking respectfully to those around you. When back talk happens, look for patterns and identify root causes. Keep an eye on what your child watches and what types of interactions he's exposed to. Some children's programming demonstrates rude, back-talk-type behavior, which kids can then feel free to imitate. Praise your child when she speaks respectfully, and thank her when she demonstrates politeness and consideration.

IN THE MOMENT

Quash the impulse to respond to your child in an equally snarky way, and continue to demonstrate respectful ways of communicating. Our children cannot develop a skill that we do not demonstrate for them, so show your child what respectful dialogue, with give and take, looks like—even if it's the last thing you feel like doing in that moment. Let your child know that you heard him and understand his feelings without giving much attention to the angry tone that it was presented with: "You must be feeling really angry right now because you're talking disrespectfully. You can be mad, but that's not an acceptable way to react." Bonus points if you can deliver this calm, cool, and collected line without clenching your fists and gritting your teeth!

WHEN THE MOMENT HAS PASSED

Though it's important to address the behavior, remember that back talk is a normal part of development. The calmer you are and the less you feed into the back talk, the less power your child's sassiness holds.

Peer Pressure

When I was in fifth grade, all the cool kids in my class wore puka shell necklaces and surfer shirts. Day after day, the "Populars" donned this uniform, most of them with tan skin and blonde hair to complement the outfits. Despite the fact that I rarely visited the beach and had never stepped onto a surfboard, I had to get my hands on a Roxy shirt. Though this was a subtle case of peer pressure, this type of thing is quite common and harmless. Unfortunately, at the other end of the spectrum are many instances that are more overt and potentially dangerous, such as pressure to smoke, drink, bully others, take excessive risks, or engage in sexual activity.

CAUSES

As kids become more aware of their desire to fit in with social groups, the influence of others becomes increasingly important. Your child's friends have likely been both subtly and overtly impacting your child's choices for a while now, but this influence tends to become more prominent as they all head into the tween and teen years. Like many children at this age, I wanted a Roxy shirt so that I could fit in with the cool kids. Sometimes children succumb to peer pressure because they're afraid of potential backlash or they feel uncomfortable being the odd man out.

PREVENTION

When we hear "peer pressure," we tend to think of it as a negative thing, such as pressure to smoke, drink, or steal. However, peers can have a positive influence as well, for instance, by encouraging a friend to join a team sport or participate in the science fair. Let your child know that you have confidence in her ability to make wise choices. As you prepare your child for possible scenarios that could be dangerous or concerning (such as pressure to drink), come up with solutions together as to how your child could handle the situation. Let your child use you as the bad guy ("My parents are so lame and will flip out if I drink!"). Come up with a word or signal that your child could use to help her get out of trouble, such as if she's at a friend's house and feels uncomfortable with something that others are doing.

IN THE MOMENT
There will likely be a time when your child does something negative due to peer pressure. When this happens, remain calm and talk with your child about what happened. Remember, these are moments for teaching your child how to handle a situation more effectively in the future. Harsh discipline and punishment translate as shame and blame to your child, making it less likely that he'll reach out to you in the future.

WHEN THE MOMENT HAS PASSED
Help your child differentiate between healthy, positive types of peer pressure and those that are potentially dangerous. Wanting trendy clothing that fits in with the kids at school is relatively harmless and to be expected, but things like drinking or smoking can be harmful. Talk with your child about ways to get out of circumstances where she feels pressured, helping her be prepared when difficult situations

arise. Remind her of the system you devised for her to let you know when she needs your help.

Bullying

When Alexa came home from school, she ran straight to her room, sobbing. Earlier that day, she discovered that her friends had drawn devil's horns and scribbled cruel names across her photo in the school yearbook. She felt crushed because she thought the other girls were her friends, and upon discovering the yearbook, she felt alone and betrayed.

Most adults can look back on their childhood and adolescence and recount at least a handful of times when they felt bullied by other kids. Whether it's physical aggression, relational aggression (like Alexa's situation), verbal attacks, social bullying, or cyberbullying, the impacts of bullying can be intense and long-lasting.

CAUSES
There are likely underlying unmet emotional needs in children who bully, potentially stemming from feeling powerless or helpless, needing attention, or wanting to gain some control in their lives. Some children who bully may come from dysfunctional and unhealthy families, where they aren't taught appropriate ways to resolve conflict. Some kids may be experiencing bullying themselves and then acting out their anger through aggression toward others. Regardless of the root causes, most children who engage in these types of behaviors struggle greatly with managing their own emotions in prosocial ways, leading them to act out aggressively or antisocially.

PREVENTION

Although it's not possible to prevent others from saying and doing hurtful things, it's important to continue to teach your child about empathy. Help him understand that some people treat other people poorly because of hard circumstances in their own lives. Help your child learn self-defense and take personal safety training so he can protect himself.

IN THE MOMENT

Because the root cause of aggressive and hostile behavior is complex and frequently stems from a range of issues, there's no quick fix. When your child tells you about bullying that she's experienced, the mama or papa bear in you may come out in full force. Try to listen calmly and thank your child for sharing with you.

Encourage your child to avoid the bully and use the buddy system, as she'll be less at risk if she has friends nearby. Help your child with cool-down strategies, like walking away from the aggressor, counting to 10, taking deep breaths, and talking to a trusted adult. Don't minimize your child's experience, but rather provide a safe space and ask open-ended questions about the incident. You can let your child know that you'll speak to someone at school who can help her navigate the situation. Report any illegal behavior, such as sexting, physical assault, or cyberbullying, to law enforcement and school officials.

WHEN THE MOMENT HAS PASSED

Because bullying can negatively impact your child's self-confidence, help your child find settings in which he can feel safe and supported, such as a youth group, sports team, or drama club. Regardless of the setting, the goal is to get your kid plugged into a peer group that provides healthy and positive support. Continue to keep the lines of communication open between you and your child.

If you are concerned about the impact of bullying on your child's mental and emotional health, consider reaching out to a mental health professional who can assist you and your child in the healing process.

A MOMENT OF SANITY

Your child is getting older, and the angst-filled years of adolescence are quickly approaching. As your child's need and desire for privacy and time away from family increases, rediscover the joys of an old hobby—whether it's reading a novel with a cup of tea, taking an afternoon bike ride, playing an instrument, or enjoying an exhilarating night out dancing. Reconnect to something you enjoy that's just for you.

BATHROOM MIRROR REMINDERS

Snap a photo of this page with your phone so you can easily reference it. You might even find it helpful to copy the page and hang these reminders on your bathroom mirror (or some other place that you see often) for quick tips when you need a refresher.

1. It's normal to feel frustrated or exasperated.

2. Don't be afraid to reach out for help.

3. Remember that your kid is a kid—and is still learning the skills to be an adult.

4. Stages (and therefore issues) don't last forever.

5. Stay calm, take a break, take a breath.

6. Get on your child's level, and use in-between times like driving in the car to connect.

7. You're *not* in control of your child's actions. You *are* in control of how you respond to your child.

8. Be clear, simple, and direct in your communication with your child.

9. Even if your kid doesn't think so, you are in fact cool.

10. Lead with love, and you'll be winning the game.

Resources

The Whole-Brain Child: 12 Revolutionary Strategies to Nurture Your Child's Developing Mind **by Daniel J. Siegel and Tina Payne Bryson:** Focusing on brain development and the typical stages that children move through, the authors outline techniques and tools to use with kids of all ages.

How to Talk So Kids Will Listen & Listen So Kids Will Talk **by Adele Faber and Elaine Mazlish:** This book helps parents learn positive communication tools to use within their home, thereby decreasing tension and stress and improving cooperation.

Siblings Without Rivalry: How to Help Your Children Live Together So You Can Live Too **by Adele Faber and Elaine Mazlish:** With too much content to fit into their previous book, *How to Talk So Kids Will Listen & Listen So Kids Will Talk*, the authors provide helpful and insightful information to help parents manage the chaos and conflict that inevitably arise between siblings.

Child of Mine: Feeding with Love and Good Sense **by Ellyn Satter:** Through understanding children's development, the author provides information on how to help kids develop positive relationships with food and eating. She explains the division of responsibility for parents and children when it comes to meals.

Peaceful Parent, Happy Siblings: How to Stop the Fighting and Raise Friends for Life **by Dr. Laura Markham:** Based on scientific research, this book helps parents navigate the challenges that come with siblings.

Pride and Joy: A Guide to Understanding Your Child's Emotions and Solving Family Problems **by Kenneth Barish, PhD:** With an emphasis on emotional attunement, this book helps parents understand their children's behaviors and discusses ways to better connect with them.

What Were You Thinking? Learning to Control Your Impulses **by Bryan Smith:** The story follows a third grader who struggles with controlling his impulses at school, sometimes hurting others' feelings in the process.

CDC: "Positive Parenting Tips"; https://www.cdc.gov /ncbddd/childdevelopment/positiveparenting/index.html. The Centers for Disease Control and Prevention (CDC) provides a helpful, easy-to-navigate web page with information on typical ages and stages, including developmental milestones, safety concerns, and guidance tips.

The Center for Parenting Education: "Temperament Rating Scales"; https://centerforparentingeducation.org/library-of -articles/child-development/temperament-rating-scales/. This website provides detailed information on the nine temperament traits that can be helpful in determining the characteristics of both you and your child.

Conscious Discipline: https://consciousdiscipline.com/. Dr. Becky Bailey is an author and educator, and the founder of Conscious Discipline. Her work is known worldwide, and there are many great resources available through her website.

Positive Discipline: "Family Meetings"; https://www. positive discipline.com/articles/family-meetings. On her website, Positive Discipline, author Jane Nelsen provides a family meeting training plan with detailed, step-by-step actions to institute with your own family.

The Prof Mom: https://www.theprofmom.com/. Through her website, Amanda hosts webinars and offers parent/teacher education.

References

Alexander, Jessica Joelle, and Iben Dissing Sandahl. *The Danish Way of Parenting: What the Happiest People in the World Know About Raising Confident, Capable Kids.* New York: TarcherPerigee, 2016.

Anderson, Laurel. *Dancing in Today's World: Effects of Socialization on the Child, Family and Community.* 2nd ed. Dubuque, IA: Kendall Hunt, 2017.

Martorell, Gabriela. *Child: From Birth to Adolescence.* New York: McGraw-Hill, 2013.

Miller, Darla Ferris. *Positive Child Guidance.* 8th ed. Boston: Cengage Learning, 2016.

Nelsen, Jane. *Positive Discipline: The Classic Guide to Helping Children Develop Self-Discipline, Responsibility, Cooperation, and Problem-Solving Skills.* New York: Ballantine, 2006.

Runkel, Hal E. *Screamfree Parenting: The Revolutionary Approach to Raising Your Kids by Keeping Your Cool.* New York: Broadway Books, 2007.

Satter, Ellyn. *Child of Mine: Feeding with Love and Good Sense.* Boulder, CO: Bull, 2000.

Thomas, Alexander, and Stella Chess. *Temperament and Development.* Oxford: Brunner/Mazel, 1977.

Index

About the Author

Amanda Hill, MEd, is a professor of child development and a parent educator. With degrees in child and adolescent development and education, as well as a background working in early childhood education, she's passionate about helping parents and teachers learn about children and their develop-  ment. Amanda lives in San Diego with her husband, Jerry, and their two children, Emery and JT. You can learn more about her and her work at www.theprofmom.com.